May 23, 1997

Teaching From
Cupboards
& Closets

Teaching From
Cupboards & Closets

Integrated Learning Activities for Young Children

by
Moira D. Green

Illustrated by
Kimble Mead

GoodYearBooks

An Imprint of ScottForesman
A Division of HarperCollins*Publishers*

DEDICATION

(My first dedication, so please indulge me.)

To my parents, Tom and Louise Green, for their fervent appreciation of creativity.

To David Black, for sharing part of his journey with me.

To Bill and June Black, for their unflagging support and faith.

To Eden Sommerville and Bobbie Dempsey, my editors, for all their help with this book.

And lastly, to my sister Deirdre, for being who she is.

GoodYearBooks
are available for most basic curriculum subjects plus many enrichment areas.
For more GoodYearBooks, contact your local bookseller or educational dealer.
For a complete catalog with information about other GoodYearBooks, please write:

GoodYearBooks
ScottForesman
1900 East Lake Avenue
Glenview, IL 60025

ISBN 0-673-36011-3

2 3 4 5 6 EQ 99 98 97 96 95

CONTENTS

(+Denotes more sophisticated language arts integration)

Section 3: FOOD

Section 4: WORK RELATED OBJECTS

Section 5: FANTASY

INTRODUCTION

I don't know anyone, parent or teacher, who feels there's enough time in the day to accomplish everything necessary. Because of the intense demands on my time, I often find myself "winging it" when I'm planning and preparing an activity to do with young kids. Some of my spontaneous (sounds so much better than "last minute") projects can turn out surprisingly well, but I never feel as good about them as the ones I've given careful thought to.

No quality curriculum for children is completely preparation-free, but it's the goal of this guide to present whole language activities for children aged three and a half to six or seven (preschoolers through first-graders) which utilize everyday, easily accessible materials and which require relatively simple preparation.

An advantage of using everyday, household materials for whole language activities is that ideally, there is already some level of familiarity with, knowledge of, and exposure to the materials and elements, so that kids can extend theme concepts during their own personal, recreation time. The units in this guide need not be used in sequential order; five food themes in a row might wear a bit thin. If you're doing a general food theme though, three or four food units would certainly be appropriate. Within each section, units graduate from those which set out to develop one or two language components through a single activity, to units with activities that develop all components of language at the same time. This allows you to start with simpler units when children are at a stage in their development where each individual component of language requires separate focus and attention, and to then move on to the more sophisticated units later, when kids have developed their language skills sufficiently to be ready for more challenging projects. The themes which utilize a multiple-skill approach are marked with a "plus" symbol in the table of contents.

Because children are so sensory-oriented, the introductory rhyme of each unit is designed to capture the sensory-related characteristics of each material or element. If you like, make a D'Nealian chart of each rhyme with very large print to help children identify individual words, as well as create a print-rich environment.

"Sensory" activities are those which make use of substances children can touch, manipulate, smell, hear and sometimes taste; in general, things they can explore with their senses. Substances used in these activities include water, gravel, buttons, noodles,

oranges, and more. You can either use a sensory table (a table with tubs that are part of the table itself), or large plastic tubs set on tables.

Within each theme, projects are divided between those which are introductory, and those which are intended to be set out around the room at various centers for child-initiated activity. One part of the whole language approach that works well for me and for other teachers I've observed, is to begin each day by gathering the children together and using literature, discussion, music, and movement to introduce the theme. Then, after the initial introductory activities, I talk briefly about the projects available in the room that day, and let the children go to work.

Children who are given the power to choose their own activities and their own ways of exploring materials are children who feel empowered. Given the fact that there are so many decisions adults make for kids every day, it's especially important to allow children free choice whenever possible. For this reason, each Attention Grabber activity is designed to make the children <u>want</u> to gather together each morning. All other activities in the guide are also based on the principle of attraction rather than coercion, in order to ensure a genuinely child-initiated program. For example, in the science activity with balls, I've suggested that you, the teacher or parent, build your own ramp, roll your own ball down it, and then talk to the children about what you're doing. By approaching the activity in this way, children can see what's happening, and make their own choice about whether or not to become involved. I always try not to feel too bad when my kids choose not to participate in a certain activity that I'm very excited about. It can really disappoint me, but I try to hold the thought that they'll explore the materials in their own way, and for that day, will learn what they need to learn.

You'll probably want to implement each theme over a period of two or three days. I always try to achieve a balance of the different curriculum areas every day, but I daily repeat the introductory activities because the repetition helps the kids learn the songs, rhymes and fingerplays. The rhymes in the guide are short enough to be used at the start of every day for the purpose of re-introducing the theme before reading something longer, like a book.

The multicultural and anti-bias emphasis of the guide is designed to underline the importance of these philosophies at home and at school. It's been my experience that both the minds and eyes of adults and children pick out differences readily enough, and this is why, it seems to me, a concentrated focus on differences tends to defeat the purpose. When children ask about the ways in which we're all different, of course I try to answer them honestly, but I also find that sameness is an important topic. The themes of this guide seek to emphasize one simple sameness of human experience; the reactions and sensations that result from experiencing some familiar household textures, materials and situations.

Sometimes, when looking for books that focus on a specific theme, I find it's extremely difficult to find those which are multicultural and anti-bias. If you have this problem also, you may find some of these options useful: if you've bought the book yourself, and the people in the illustrations are all white, you can color in diverse skin shades. Some educators feel that this encourages children to draw in books, but I've never experienced this. If the book has been borrowed from the library, say something to the kids after reading it like: "You know, I really liked that story. There's one thing I don't like about it, though. Everyone in it has pink skin, and in the real world, people have all kinds of different skin colors. I wish the people in this book were drawn the way people in the world look."

HOW TO USE THIS BOOK

The picture activity signs and writing sheets have several purposes: they help create a print-rich environment, provide reading and writing opportunities, and present symbols and words that are directly related to what children are experiencing and exploring. A picture activity sign uses words and symbols to suggest ways to use the materials. For each picture sign, write the suggested directions for the activity or some of your own, including pictures or rebus symbols above as many words as possible to help younger children decipher the instructions. A writing sheet gives kids the chance to record what they counted, discovered or observed during a particular project.

Since it's important that your signs and sheets reflect the sizes and shapes of materials you're actually using, you will be drawing them yourself. Some samples are included here to provide a general format, NOTE and the clip art section will help you with drawing your pictures. Descriptions of both signs and sheets are included within the units as well. I suggest using the D'Nealian print chart as a guide for lettering. It's very important to draw a picture above as many words as you can. The more pictures you include, the easier it is for children to connect written words with their meanings. For example, for numbers, you can write the word, the numeral and the corresponding number of dots beside it to aid comprehension. Again, illustration samples of commonly used rebus words are included in the clip art section.

These reading and writing activities are especially appropriate for later in the year, when writing skills are more developed, or for a group of children who already spend a lot of their time copying and writing letters, asking how words are spelled, and who are clearly ready to take the next step. Younger children do enjoy scribbling on the writing sheets, and do sometimes recognize the symbols as being related to the experiences. It's important to encourage invented spelling, another integral step in the process.

The writing sheets are intended to be available for children who <u>want</u> to use them, but are by no means something children should be required to do. It's a good idea to also provide blank paper for those who want to take writing in another direction. I usually put pens, not pencils or crayons, with writing sheets because the kids I teach seem to feel it gives their work more importance. The fact that adults almost always use pens is not lost on them!

Some of us are in contact with preschoolers who already read, and many kindergartners have this ability. After a day's theme activities, I've often seen these children approach the theme posters and charts on the walls, and read everything written there. This is why I try to have as many large print posters and charts on the walls as I can, and to place them at the children's eye level whenever possible. This includes charts the children have written themselves, and charts on which I've taken their dictation. Dictation accomplishes several valuable goals: it helps the children see that their words are important, that their ideas have form and shape through the written word, and perhaps most importantly, that their original

thought is communicated every time someone reads their words.

Teachers' use of their own sample art is a controversial issue. Some educators feel that samples inhibit children's creativity, and that they encourage kids to imitate the work of adults. I find that when I omit sample art, children often sit waiting at the table until they can ask me what to do with the materials, and generally seem less interested in the activity. When I use samples, children will often literally stampede over to the art table, and seem much more excited about the project. It is a good idea though, to remark, "This is just the project <u>I</u> made. Everyone's work will look different because each of us is different and special."

All of us know that teaching and parenting can be tremendously rewarding and fun, but also incredibly hard, and sometimes frustrating, work. I hope these activity ideas make working with kids just a little easier. Lastly, I recommend never taking any child development theory or teaching approach too seriously. If you love kids by respecting them, attending to them, and cherishing them, your teaching — whatever method you use — will be the best gift it can be.

Teaching From

Household Objects

Balls

Spools

Cylinders

Buttons

Boppy bouncy
jounce and jump,
rubber balls
that bop and bump.

THEME: balls

In order to have as many differently shaped, sized, and colored balls as possible for this theme, you can ask the children ahead of time to bring their balls from home. You may also need to remind parents when it's ball day, and you may want to ask if you can write names on balls with a marker. Alternatively, you can be prepared with name stickers for the large balls. If you're a parent at home, you might ask if you can borrow some balls from your neighbors. The more balls you have, the better. Many-sided balls and small, rubber balls of varying colors and sizes are available at independent toy stores and at some chains. If you have a plastic pool, large garbage container, or other large tub, designate it as the place for balls when the children aren't playing with them.

INTRODUCTORY ACTIVITIES

Attention Grabber
Go to a place in your home or classroom which is away from the activities you've prepared. As the children arrive, tell them you have

something behind your back, and you're wondering if they can guess what it is. As you wait for everyone to arrive, give the children clues, and when everyone is gathered, take a ball from behind your back and let them pass it around. Tip: The more interesting the ball, (multi-colored, many-sided) the better!

INTRODUCTORY DISCUSSION

objective   Introduce the theme; develop speaking and listening skills.

materials   Ball rhyme; any pictures or drawings of balls you've been able to obtain; and, depending on how long the children are able to remain physically inactive, one of the books listed at the end of this unit.

directions   After reading the ball rhyme, count the number of balls in the illustration as a group. Ask questions like: Are all the balls the same shape? What ball games do you play at home? Using the ball rhyme, drawings, or other books in the same way, encourage the children to describe their experiences with, and observations of balls.

MOVEMENT:
Being A Ball

objective   [*Onomatopoeia*: the formation of a word by imitating the natural sound associated with the object or action involved.]   Coordinate gross motor activity with onomatopoeic rhyme and help children "feel" language.

materials   Open space.

directions   Say each word in the ball rhyme and as you do, ask the children to move in the way that the word sounds: boppy, bouncy, jounce, jump, bop, bump. (Caution: before you say the word "bump," ask the children: "Is it O.K. for us to bump into each other? What will happen if we do?")

MOVEMENT/MUSIC:
We Are Rubber:

objective   Help children feel comfortable singing; facilitate gross motor development.

materials   Your voices

To the tune of Frere Jacques:
We are rubber, we are rubber,
See us bounce, see us bounce,
bouncy bouncy bounce bounce
bouncy bouncy bounce bounce
bounce bounce bounce
bounce bounce bounce.

directions   For movement, you can begin bouncing your
fingers, then fists, then finally you and the children
can curl up like balls and bounce your
whole bodies.

ACTIVITY CENTERS

ART/GROSS MOTOR:
Ball Painting

objective   Develop motor skills; facilitate fun with paint and balls!

materials   Several large balls
Large strips of butcher paper
Several large, shallow pans
Rocks to act as paperweights on a windy day
Paint - a different color for each pan
Smocks
Tubs of soapy water — two
Paper towels
Garbage can
Also: You'll want to use the materials for the "Our Balls" Chart
in the language activity below while the kids are waiting for turns.

preparation   Find a large asphalt or cement area outdoors, and spread your butcher paper
strips out on the ground. Use a rock on either end of each strip if it's a gusty
day. Place the pans of paint at each end of each strip, and put a ball in each
pan. Nearby, place the smocks, one tub of soapy water, paper towels, and the
garbage can. At another spot, place the other tub of soapy water by itself.

directions   Invite the children to swish the balls around in the pans of paint, and then to
roll them along the butcher paper. Usually, not all of the ball gets covered with
paint. Ask children why the ball doesn't make an unbroken painted line.
Show the children the tub of water by itself, and explain that when the ball

rolls on the ground and gets dirty, they can wash it off in the tub. Encourage the children to use the soapy water, towels and garbage can when they're finished with their part of the ball painting.

LANGUAGE:
"Our Balls" Chart

objective Facilitate the understanding that spoken words can be put in written form; develop speaking skills.

materials One large piece of butcher paper
One black and one blue marker

preparation Spread the butcher paper out on a table which is central to the area where children are participating in the ball painting.

directions As children wait their turn to paint, pick one of these questions and ask it of each child: What's your favorite game to play with a ball?; Tell me about your ball; or, Do you have a ball at home? What does it look like? For 3's and 4's you can write down their dictated answers. It's best to use printscript or D'Nealian rather than cursive so that kids can identify individual words more easily. As you write the answers, use two marker colors, and alternate the color for each sentence so that children can easily identify complete sentences. Use quotation marks, and write the child's name after her/his answer. Children who are 5 and over often want to do their own writing. If necessary, write their answers out clearly on another piece of paper, so that they can copy them onto the chart. If time permits, say each word as they write it. When the chart is finished, find a good spot on the wall for it, and read the chart to the children the next morning during introductory activities, or at another time when they're gathered together.

ART:
Ball Chart

objective Facilitate creative expression; develop fine motor skills through drawing, cutting and gluing.

materials The chart made in the preceding activity
Markers or crayons
Toy catalogs
Children's scissors
Glue or glue sticks

preparation Spread all materials out on the table.

directions As each child approaches, read the child's sentence on the chart from the language activity below, and ask her/him if s/he would like to draw a picture of her/his ball, or find a picture of a ball in the catalogs to cut out and glue onto the chart.

Tip: If you use toy catalogs, talk to the children about the biased representation there may be in some of them. Some commonly show only girls using housekeeping toys, only boys engaged in physically aggressive or rowdy play, only boys using science equipment, only boys in dress-up costumes that represent daring and courage, only girls in costumes that represent the helping professions, only token representatives of diverse cultures, and no children with disabilities. If you have catalogs like these, look at them together and ask questions like: "Are girls the only ones who play in housekeeping?; Are boys the only ones who can be cowboys?; I notice that almost all of the children in this catalog have pink skin. Do you think all of the children in the world have pink skin?" and so forth.

SCIENCE:
Ball Bounce Experiment

objective Facilitate the understanding that smooth balls bounce differently than many-sided ones; develop scientific observation; develop speaking skills.

materials As many many-sided balls as possible that are the same size.
As many regular balls as possible that are roughly the same size as the many-sided ones.
An open space

preparation Tell the children that you have a science experiment for them, and take them to an open space. Put the balls in a place easily accessible to them.

directions Encourage the children to bounce both kinds of balls. Invite them to express their hypotheses and findings. Encourage them to predict where or how a regular ball will bounce, and where or how a many-sided ball will bounce. Are they different? Why?

SCIENCE/SENSORY:
Ball Float Experiment

objective Facilitate the understanding that balls float, and that some float because they're rubber while others float because they're filled with air; provide sensory experience with water and balls.

materials Rubber balls
Air-filled balls
Tubs or sensory table filled with water
One small rubber ball cut cleanly in half
One deflated air ball
Activity sign
Steel balls and marbles

preparation Write a picture sign that says: "Would you like to try to sink the balls?" and hang it near the project.

directions Encourage the kids to explore and experiment. Show them the device on air-filled balls through which air is pumped. As they try to sink the balls, talk to them about what they discover.
Encourage older children to contrast and compare the steel and marble balls with the rubber and air-filled ones. Which ball is heaviest? What is inside each ball? What is each ball made of? Why isn't it hard to sink the marble and steel balls?

SCIENCE:
Ball Roll Experiment

objective Facilitate exploration and observation of the relationship between height and distance.

materials Blocks
Ramps
Balls

preparation Place the balls in the block area.

directions Build a ramp yourself, and roll your ball down it. Say: "Wow! Look! I made a ramp and my ball rolled really far! I wonder what'll happen if I use less/more blocks under my ramp — I wonder if my ball will roll farther, or not as far." When the children begin to experiment with their own ramps, write their names on masking tape strips so they can mark how far their ball rolled. If appropriate or pertinent, talk about the relationship between a high ramp and far-rolling ball, and a low ramp and short-rolling ball.

MATH:
Roll Measure Chart - continued from previous activity

objective Facilitate understanding of comparable distances; provide experience with graphs; facilitate measuring.

materials   Large piece of butcher paper or cardboard
Blocks
Markers - as many different colors as possible
Measuring tape
Rulers

preparation   Write each child's name at the head of a column, using a differently colored marker for each one.

directions   After the children mark how far their balls rolled, invite them to measure that distance. Show them how to put several blocks of the same size end to end and measure the distance the ball rolled. After measuring the distance, each child can trace the shape of the block in the column under her/his name, color in the block, and next to it, write the number of blocks s/he counted in measuring how far the ball rolled.

Also, have rulers and measuring tapes available for casual use, and point out the inches and feet on them if appropriate. When measuring distance with blocks, kindergartners can be encouraged to measure several times, using a differently shaped or sized block each time. Then, on the chart, they can compare the number of each block needed for the same distance. If you like, you can talk about what the chart shows during the next morning's introductory activities. If you're at home, and don't have access to blocks, use any other manipulative toy you have which is comprised of same sized, fairly large pieces.

MATH:
Ball Drop Game

objective   Facilitate rational counting; develop fine motor skills; promote self-esteem and autonomy through a one-person work station.

materials   One large coffee can with lid
Two toilet paper rolls or other cardboard tubes
As many small balls as possible that will fit through the cardboard tubes.
A box or container large enough to hold balls
Photocopies of writing sheet in appendix
A pen
A razor blade or exacto knife

preparation For easier tracing, cut one toilet paper roll so that it's only about one inch tall. Put the end of it on the plastic coffee can lid, and trace around the inside of it. With a razor blade or exacto knife, cut the hole out and trim it so that the uncut toilet paper roll fits through it exactly without being loose. Push it down about a quarter of the way. If you have time, cover the can and the cardboard tube with some pretty or exciting paper. Place it at a small table, and put the box or container of balls next to it. On a stiff piece of paper, draw one stick figure, the number 1, and the words: "One person may be here." Lower down on the sign, write: "Would you like to count the balls?" Place the sign at the table. For older children, also put ball count writing sheets and pens on the table.

directions Encourage each child to drop each ball down the tube into the coffee can, and to count each one as s/he does. Kids can write down the number of each color of ball on the writing sheets.

SOCIAL STUDIES:
Ball Wash

objective Facilitate the understanding that some jobs require cooperation between two people.

materials
    One big ball
    One tub of soapy water
    One scrub brush or rag
    One sign

preparation Put the biggest ball you can find, which is likely to be the most slippery when wet, in a big tub of soapy water. Put a scrub brush or dish rag next to the tub, also. Above the tub, place a sign that says: "Slippery Ball Wash. Wash the ball by yourself, or with a friend. Which is easiest?"

directions Read the sign to the children when they ask you what it says. If young children need support in asking a friend to help them, ask if they would like you to ask the friend for them. Encourage them to try both ways of washing the ball. Ask: "What happens when you try to wash the ball by yourself?" and "What happens when someone holds it for you?" Praise each child's cleaning and washing of the ball: "Look how clean you're getting it!" and also the child who's holding it: "Lindsay's holding it so still for you!" By doing this, each child can feel good about individual accomplishment even though the activity is a cooperative effort.

DRAMATIC PLAY:
Toy Store

objective   Facilitate imaginative, creative play; develop speaking skills; facilitate interaction between children.

materials   Tables and shelves
Toys, including lots of balls
Pictures of toys
Signs advertising specials and sale items
Receipt notebook
Pens
Paper bags
Toy cash registers
Money — either pretend or real pennies

preparation   Hang the advertisements and pictures of toys from the catalogs on the wall. Items like these contribute to a print-rich environment. It's fun to try to think of, and acquire, as many materials as you can that accomplish this (i.e. telephone books, order forms, letterhead paper and so forth.) When I've explained what I want them for, I've often had good luck in getting materials like these donated by stores and other businesses. This really helps the children's dramatic play process because it allows them to use materials that are "the real thing." Ask the kids what a good name for the toy store would be, make a sign with them, and put it up.

directions   Encourage the children to explore, and to play in the toy store. Pretend to be a customer, or use one of the telephones to call the store with a question.

EXTENDING THE CONCEPT

speaking and listening skills Have a show and tell with the balls the kids have brought from home. With young 3's or very large groups, split up into two groups so that children don't have to sit still for very long.

listening skills One morning, after singing the We Are Rubber song, put some music on the record player or tape recorder, and have the children sit in a circle. Roll a ball across to the person on the other side. Tell the children to pretend that the ball is very hot, and that they can only touch it long enough to roll it to someone else. This will keep the ball moving. When the music stops, the ball turns icy, and the person holding it freezes like a statue until the music starts again. With older children, use more than one ball.

math/ cognitive skills Place the balls the kids brought from home in a container near a long strip of butcher paper. Stick masking tape circles or double-sided tape all along the paper strip so balls don't roll away as easily. At the top of the butcher paper make a picture sign that says: "Would you like to line up the balls from smallest to biggest?"

gross motor Put a different twist on ball bouncing on a hot summer day. Fill a pool a third or half way full with water. Put masking tape all around the pool, about two or three feet from the pool's edge, depending on how wet you want the children to get. Put big balls in the water. Kids can stand at the tape line, and bounce the balls into the water. The kids on the other side of the pool catch them. This is a fun way to stay cool on a hot day, but watch out for big splashes!

science When the children are experimenting with how far balls roll down ramps, encourage them to compare rolling a ball down a ramp with rolling it up by using a big wooden plank if you have one. Ask, "Why does the ball roll down every time and never all the way up?" Explain that the earth pulls things towards itself, and that the name for this is gravity.

LITERATURE

*Denotes multicultural and/or anti-bias.

I like to use Tana Hoban's books by saying to the children before I start: "Somewhere in this book there's a ball (or spool, or cylinder etc.) so let's keep our eyes open to see if we can spot it."

*Bang, Molly, *Yellow Ball*, Morrow Junior Books, 1991

*Clifton, Lucille, *My Friend Jacob*, E. P. Dutton, 1980

*Hoban, Tana, *Is it larger? Is it smaller?*, Greenwillow, 1985

*Hoban, Tana, *Shadows and Reflections*, Macmillan, 1990

Sis, Peter, *Beach Ball*, Greenwillow, 1990

Tafuri, Nancy, *The Ball Bounced*, Greenwillow, 1989

Spillable spools,
some big
and some little;
runaway rollers,
with holes
in the middle.

THEME: spools

There are so many imaginative things you can do with spools, and as with all collections, the more you have, and the greater variety, the better. Nowadays, most adults have too little time to make clothes from scratch, but even the busiest parent still mends a small tear or sews a button back on. At such times, children notice the sewing spool that's used, and hopefully will recognize this item when you bring it out and introduce your theme.

INTRODUCTORY ACTIVITIES

Attention Grabber

Find your quiet spot away from the activities, and hide a box of spools behind your back. As the children approach, tell them you have something behind your back and that you have one for everyone. Give them hints until all children arrive, then bring out the box. Pass it around and let every child take a spool to hold.

INTRODUCTORY DISCUSSION

objective Introduce the theme to children; develop speaking skills; develop listening skills.

materials	Spool rhyme A spool with thread on it A stick that fits through the spool
directions	After the Attention Grabber activity, read the spool rhyme at least twice. Ask the children, "Have you ever seen spools before? Where? What are they used for?" Show the children the spool with the thread on it. Explain that a sewing machine has a special place for the thread that is like the stick. Put the spool on the stick, and pull the thread so that the spool turns. Then, as you pull the thread, ask the children what the spool is doing.

MUSIC/MOVEMENT:
The Spool Song

objective	Help children feel comfortable using their singing voices; facilitate gross motor development.
materials	Open space To the tune of Row, row, row your boat: As all the thread comes off, the spool, it turns around; then when all the thread is gone it rolls along the ground.
directions	Sing the song first as a fingerplay. Use your pointing finger for the spool. For "As all the thread comes off, the spool, it turns around," use the fingers of your other hand to pull the imaginary thread, and move spool finger in circular motion. For "then when all the thread is gone," put both hands out in a 'no more left' gesture. For "it rolls along the ground," twiddle both pointing fingers around each other horizontally. For body motions, use whole body as turning spool, and turn around and around, then roll on the floor horizontally for "it rolls along the ground."

ACTIVITY CENTERS

ART:
Spool People And Their Houses

objective	Facilitate creative thinking and creative expression; develop cognition by identifying body parts and where they are located; facilitate fine motor skills.

materials
Spools
Pipe cleaners
Styrofoam balls
Glue
Fabric scraps
Paper scraps
Shoe boxes
Markers
Small boxes or small pieces of wood
Glue
Glue brushes
Yarn
Paper cups
Optional: Paper shapes (described below)

preparation
Ahead of time, make a few spool people by gluing heads on spools, using either the triangle shapes, or styrofoam balls for the heads. Draw faces on them, and glue yarn on for hair. It's important that teaching tools also reflect a multicultural approach. In a project like this, where art creations are intended to represent people, it's desirable to vary the skin shades of the figures. (Yes, even spool people are culturally diverse!) Glue pipe cleaners to wrap around the back so that there is an arm on each side. Use fabric scraps for clothes. For one spool house, use a shoe box, and use paper cups, small boxes, more spools, blocks of wood, or whatever you have handy, to make furniture. You may want to cut out most of one cardboard wall for easier access. It's also fun to cut a doorway and windows in the sides of the box with an exacto knife. Put fabric scraps on the floor for rugs or carpeting and, if you have beds, use fabric scraps as blankets. You can draw furniture inside your shoe box, also. Have all the materials listed above available on a table for the children. OPTIONAL PAPER SHAPES: Directions for making two-dimensional, paper curlicues, triangles, accordions, and discs.

Curlicues:

Cut out a circle about two or three inches in diameter. Starting on the outside of the circle, cut into the inside, around and around, to the center of the circle, so that you are making a spiral. When you're finished, pull up the middle to make a curlicue that looks like a paper spring. You can vary these measurements to suit yourself, and to create curlicues of different sizes.

Triangles:

Cut out a piece of construction paper that's 7" long, and 1 and 1/2 inches wide. Fold the strip of paper into three equal 2" segments, with one 1" inch segment left over. Arrange the three segments into a triangle, and staple the one inch flap onto the 2" segment it overlaps.
You can vary the measurements to suit yourself, and to create triangles of different dimensions.

Accordions:

Cut out a strip of paper about 10" long and 1/2" wide. Measure about 1 and 1/2" of one end, and fold that much forward. Fold the same amount back, the same amount forward and so on until the entire strip is folded into an accordion shape. Again, vary the measurements to suit yourself.

Discs:

Cut out a circle about 3" in diameter. Cut a straight line from the outside of the circle to the center. Pull both of the cut edges together until they overlap, and then staple them. When you do this, you should be left with a disc that's convex or concave, depending on which way you turn it.

directions   While the children are gathered for the day's introductory activities, show them the spool people and their house, and tell them the story on page 20, or a story of your own. When you've finished the story, ask them what they see on the table. Then ask them what they could do with the materials. If your kids are like the children I've taught, they'll suggest that you make spool people and spool houses. If you get another suggestion though, go with it! If your children make spool people, talk about the parts of their bodies as the children make them: head, arms, eyes, mouth, hair and so forth.

ART:
Spool Carriers

objective   Develop problem solving skills; develop self-esteem and sense of autonomy by providing opportunities for choice; develop fine motor skills.

materials
Plastic strawberry baskets
Yarn or string
Spools
Fabric
Glitter
Glue
Glue brushes
Tacks
Masking tape
Optional: paper curlicues, triangles and discs
    from pages 17 and 18 or described above

preparation   In this activity, yarn attached to two walls acts as a transit line, and strawberry baskets slide along them. You'll probably want to leave the project up for a few days, so choose a corner which will be convenient for you. Wrap each end of the yarn or string lengths in masking tape for easy threading through the spools, later. Using a tack or tape, attach or tie one end of the yarn at a place on one wall, and string it across the corner at an angle. Attach the other end to the other wall. Make sure the yarn is at a height the children can reach. Repeat all steps with another piece of yarn, but string it at a different angle, and make sure there is at least a foot and a half between transit lines, so that spool carriers traveling along the upper yarn line will not get caught on the one below. Decorate a fruit basket with collage materials. Thread two sections of yarn of equal length through one spool. Tie each end of one yarn length to opposite ends of the fruit basket, and do the same with the other length. Detach one end of a transit line, and thread the spool onto it. Reattach the transit line to the wall after the spool carrier is threaded on, and then put some spool people inside your carrier.

directions Move the carrier you made up and down the transit line, and say: "Look! The spool people are going on a trip." Have all the above materials available on a nearby table, show them to the children, and ask them what they can do with them. For 3's and 4's, have the children pick out their own spools and have them decorate their own baskets, but be prepared to thread the spools, and to tie the yarn ends to the corners of the baskets yourself. Kindergartners will be able to do all steps themselves if the yarn lengths for the carriers also have masking tape ends for easy threading. When the children are ready to use their carriers, ask: "How do you think we can get your carrier onto the transit line?"

Encourage them to examine each end of the transit lines to see how they are attached and how they can be detached. Let them know it's O.K. to detach an end, and to thread it through the spool of their carriers. If needed, help them reattach the transit lines. If you've used tacks, the easiest way is to hold the yarn while the child pushes the tack in.

ART: Spool Dip

objective Develop fine motor skills; facilitate the understanding that the shape of an object influences the print it makes; facilitate creative expression through art; foster an appreciation of art.

materials Paint containers
Three colors of paint
Spools of varying diameters
Paper
Adult scissors

preparation Spread newspaper or a table cloth over your work surface. Arrange the containers of paint on the table in such a way that all children will have access to all colors. Place the spools near the containers. When you put paper out for this activity, you may want to cut it into different, interesting shapes that vary from the standard rectangular shape.

directions Encourage the children to take the spools, dip them into the paint, and make spool prints by stamping the ends of the spools. The kids may also want to roll their spools in the paint and over the paper. If this is the case, let them experiment with that. With spools that are noticeably different in diameter, make a game out of matching each print with each spool after the spool prints dry.

LANGUAGE/DRAMATIC PLAY:
Spool Community

objective Facilitate expression of ideas; expand vocabulary; develop conversational skills; facilitate fantasy play.

materials Spool people and houses made by you and the kids
Spool carriers and transit lines

preparation Spread out the spool people and their houses somewhere near the transit lines, either on the floor or on a table.

directions Tell the children the story below. Invite the children to play with the materials. On a work surface near one of the transit lines (strawberry basket carriers on yarn lines) prop a ramp (a piece of cardboard, a long wooden block, or whatever else you have handy) up on a small box to simulate a mountain for the spool people. Put the spool people in their shoe box house, around the small box that serves as the kitchen table.

story One evening when the spool family were having dinner, Momma Spool said, "It's such a beautiful evening. Let's go for a trip after dinner." So after dinner the spool family climbed into their spool car (Put the spool family in a strawberry basket and move the basket slowly along the yarn line, towards the mountain.) and went for a trip. "Oooh," Little Boy Spool said, "Look down there!" The ground was very far away. Soon, the Spool Family came to a mountain.

(Take the spool people out of the strawberry basket, and put them at the bottom of the ramp.) "Shall we climb the mountain?" Daddy Spool asked. "If we climb up, will we be able to climb down?" Little Boy Spool asked. "If we hike up, will we be able to hike down?" Momma Spool asked. "If we scramble up, will we be able to scramble down?" Little Girl Spool asked. They all decided to find out, so they climbed and hiked and scrambled up the mountain. (Move the spool people up along the ramp to the top.) When they got to the top, they looked around and wandered everywhere and explored the whole mountain. Soon they were ready to go home. (Put spool people at the edge of the ramp.)

"Oooh," Daddy Spool said, "Was the mountain this steep when we were climbing up?" "Oooh," Momma Spool said, "Was the mountain this high when we were hiking up?" "Oooh," Little Boy Spool said, "Was the mountain this big when we were scrambling up?" "I know what we'll do!" Little Girl Spool exclaimed. She wrapped her arms around herself (Fold the pipecleaner arms around the spool) and she rolled right down the mountain. (Roll the spool down the mountain.) And she went roly poly roly poly roly poly. "I think I'll try that!" Daddy Spool said. (Roll the Daddy spool down the ramp.) And he went roly poly roly poly roly poly. "I think I'll try that!" Little Boy Spool said. (Roll the boy spool down the ramp.) And he went roly poly roly poly roly poly. "Well, I have to try it, too!" Momma Spool said. (Roll mother spool down ramp.) And she went roly poly roly poly roly poly.

Then they all climbed back in their spool car to go home. (Put all the spools back in the strawberry basket.) "Oooh," Little Girl Spool said, "everything down there is so far away." And she looked out over the side of the car. (Move the strawberry basket slowly back towards the shoebox house.) When they got home, (Put the spools back in their shoebox house) Daddy Spool fixed hot chocolate with marshmallows for everybody and they all sat in the kitchen to drink it. (Move the father spool around the kitchen) Then they tucked themselves into their snug little beds (Put the spools under a fabric scrap to simulate a bed cover) and dreamed about mountains all night long.

LANGUAGE:
Spool Badges

objective	Develop speaking skills
materials	Sticky labels Scissors Marker
preparation	Using the pattern shown at on page 22, make spool badges. Write on each one: 'I bet you can't guess what I did with spools today!'
directions	Put a spool badge on yourself. Color it brightly to attract more attention, but use a light color that won't obscure the message on your badge. When the children notice and ask about it, read what it says to them, and initiate a conversation around the badge's message. Have the other badges on a tray on a table, and ask them if they'd like one. Let them peel off the backing and

put it on themselves. For older children, have blank badges and pens available in case they want to write their own message on their badges.

GROSS MOTOR:
Spool Roll

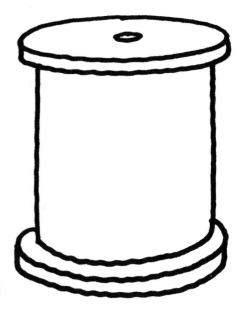

objective   Develop gross motor skills; develop hand/eye coordination.

materials   Masking tape
Spools

preparation   Using masking tape, make circles on the floor of varying sizes (from about 6" in diameter to 1'6"). Also with tape, designate spots from which the children may stand and roll their spools into the circles. Place the standing lines closer to the circles for younger children.

directions   Encourage the children to roll their spools into the circles from the line. Give them sincere praise while they participate in this activity, whether or not their spools reach the circles.

SENSORY:
Spool Cargo

objective   Facilitate sensory experience with sand or gravel and spools; develop language as children interact during sensory play.

materials   Sensory table or tubs
Sand, gravel or fish aquarium gravel
Toy dump trucks
Spools

preparation   Place sand or gravel, dump trucks and spools in the sensory table or tubs.

directions   Stand back and watch the kids play!

MATH:
Spool Counting Posts

objective   Facilitate rational counting; develop self-esteem and sense of autonomy through one-person work station; develop fine motor skills.

materials
Spools
Bamboo shish kebob skewers or other sticks that fit through spools
Styrofoam blocks (cut from large appliance styrofoam packing pieces)
Glue
Scissors
A sign
Writing sheets
Pens
Optional: A thin rod which is longer than the skewers, and
will fit through spools

preparation
In this activity you're going to be making upright posts
for the kids to slide spools onto, while they count how
many spools fit onto each post. Using a knife, cut the
styrofoam packing pieces into blocks, about 3 1/2" by
3 1/2". Take a bamboo skewer and cut off one sharp
end. Using the remaining sharp end, push the skewer
into the middle of a styrofoam block until 2 1/2" of the
skewer is in the block. Try to push it in so that the
skewer stands as straight as possible. If you want to
reinforce it, take the skewer out, dip 2 1/2" in glue,
and then put the glued end back into the block and let
it dry. Repeat this with the other two skewers, but cut
them off in such a way that one post is longest, one
shorter, and one very short. Place these on a small,
one-person table, and put a container of spools next
to them. On a sign, draw one stick figure, the
number 1, and the words: "One person may be here."
Lower down on the sign, write: "Would you like to
count how many spools fit onto each post?" Talk to
the children about how important it is to leave the
posts where they are, and to not carry them around
the room. For older students, use the very long rod
to make a giant post on which many, many spools will
fit. It will probably have to be placed on the floor. For
a base for the extra long spool post, put wet sand in
a coffee can, make a hole in the coffee lid with
scissors, and stick the post down through the lid
and through the sand. Make a sign that asks, "How
many spools fit on the big post? Take 5 away. How many spools are left?"
Provide writing sheets on which the children can write down how many spools
they counted or subtracted.

directions
Read the signs to the children when they ask what they say. Ask them about
their findings, and encourage them to describe their process of counting and

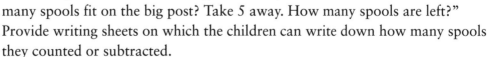

sliding spools onto posts as they work through the activities. Ask children about their findings as they work through the subtraction problem on the sign by the large post.

MATH:
Spool Sorting

objective   Facilitate sorting and counting.

materials   Spools
Sorting trays or sectioned dinner trays
Regular trays or shallow containers
Large zip lock bags
Rubbing alcohol
Food coloring — 4 colors

preparation   In a large zip lock bag, put a number of wooden spools, a few tablespoons of rubbing alcohol, a tablespoon of food coloring, and then zip the bag closed. Shake the bag so that all the spools are covered with the solution, and then leave them to soak for about half an hour. Do the same with the rest of the spools until you have four colors of spools. Let the spools dry on paper towels overnight. For the activity, set out the empty sorting trays, and also regular trays that hold a variety of the colored spools. If you don't have commercial sorting trays, you can make your own with sectioned dinner trays; cardboard or plastic, or using rubber cement, glue containers together that are uniform in size.

directions   It's my experience that some 3- and 4-year old children don't really know what to do with sorting materials, and that they need a little help grasping the concept. For this reason, there's a sorting story below which, after I've told it to my kids, can sometimes initiate a veritable sorting frenzy. Tell the story during your introductory activities and then find a safe place to stand.

story   Once upon a time there were many spool families living together, willy nilly, all a-jumble, and there was no room for anyone to do anything. One day the mother in the orange spool family said, "I'm going to go look for a new place to live. There just isn't enough room for all these spool families to live together." (Take an orange spool out.) So she went looking and looking (move spool around edges of sorting tray) and finally she found a place. "This would make a wonderful place to live!" she said. (Put spool in empty section of sorting tray.) She called to her husband and children: "Come see the new place I found to live." And so they did, and they liked it so much that they stayed. (Move all orange spools to new section.) Well, the father of the green spool family saw how happy the orange spools were in their new home, so he decided to look for a new place to live. (Take green spool out, move around edges of sorting tray, and repeat the same procedure as followed for the orange spool. Continue with each color of spool until all are sorted.)

MATH
Spool Classification Chart

objective Facilitate reading skills; facilitate the opportunity for children to express in picture format the results they discover through comparing, counting, and classifying.

materials Graph chart
Markers
Spools

preparation Classification involves sorting (separating) and grouping (joining). Older children can participate in creating the chart format, but for 3's and 4's, it's best to prepare it yourself, ahead of time. Look at all the spools, and see how many ways they can be classified — for example, are there very small ones, significantly larger ones, spools with thread still on them, differently colored spools, spools made of wood, plastic, or styrofoam? Encourage kindergartners to work through this process with you, to find all the ways that your spools are alike and different. On your chart, make a column for each of these, and in addition to drawing a symbol representing that type of spool, write a description next to it.

directions While the children are playing in the block area (see social studies activity below) bring the chart and marker over, and put them on the floor. Invite the kids to help you make a graph of all the spools. Usually children will eventually become interested and involved, but if not, complete the chart and put it up on the wall at the children's eye-level. Talk about it during the next morning's introductory activities.

SCIENCE
Rollers Or Wheels?

objective Facilitate exploration with wheels and rollers as a means of transportation; facilitate comparison of efficiency of each; develop sense of autonomy through one-person work station.

materials Toy pick-up truck or dump truck
Pebbles or small manipulatives for transporting
Rectangular styrofoam tray (meat tray)
Four spools, preferably the same size and type
Large piece of butcher paper

String
Hole punch
Popsicle stick
Markers
Toy buildings
Activity sign
"One Person May Be Here" sign

preparation   In this activity you're going to use the styrofoam tray and spools to make a rolling contraption for the children to compare with a toy vehicle that uses wheels. Spread the butcher paper out on a table such that the paper lies as flat as possible. If you have toy buildings, put them at opposite ends of the paper, and draw a road between them. If you don't have toy buildings, draw a pond at one end of the paper, and a parking lot at the other, with a road between them. Punch two holes about four inches away from each other close to the edge of the styrofoam tray's shorter sides. With two equal lengths of string, tie one end of each string length through a hole, and one end of each string length to the popsicle stick, so that you've made a pulling handle like a wagon would have. Place this, the toy dump truck, and the pebbles in the parking lot, or, if you have a toy building, place them near that. Place the styrofoam tray on the spools. On your sign, draw the pictures and write the words: "Would you like to take the pebbles to the pond/house? Try it with wheels, and try it with rollers!" Also, place your "One Person May Be Here" sign in a prominent place.

directions   Read the activity sign to the children if they ask you what it says, and discuss the pictures with them. Encourage them to express their findings. How did the truck with wheels work? How did the tray with rollers work?

SOCIAL STUDIES:
Special Builders

objective   Facilitate an understanding of the concept of specialized jobs; help understanding of specialized workers contributing to one outcome; promote cooperative play.

materials Blocks, or if you don't have blocks at home, large manipulatives.
Spools
Poster or large picture of city buildings showing as many different building parts as possible: bridges, pillars, ramps, steps, etc.
Small pictures of the same building parts from magazines
Small box
Masking or double-sided tape

preparation Pin up the poster or picture near the area where you'll be building. (If I can't find the type of poster I need, I often make one from pictures in magazines. You may have to do the same.) Mount the pictures of bridges, pillars, ramps and walls that you found from magazines on construction paper badges, and write the name of the building element below the picture on each badge. Take one, and putting masking tape on the back in order to make a badge, place it on yourself. Decorate the small box as interestingly as you can if you have time, and put the other badges inside the box. Put the box by the blocks and spools, and nearby, have several masking tape curls stuck onto the edge of a table or shelf.

directions Start to build whatever building part is designated by your badge. Tell the children: "I have a game in this box. Does anyone want to play?" As the children approach, have them pick out badges, and using the masking tape curls, help them put the badges on themselves. Talk to them about what is pictured and written on their badges, and about what they'll be building. Point out the building parts on the poster to give them a sense of how the parts work together, and let the kids get to work. When they're all finished, ask how they could connect everything together to make it one city. Older children will be more likely to spontaneously build a common structure together than 3's and 4's. After the project, talk about the different jobs you all had. This is rather a controlled activity, and although some kids really enjoy it sometimes, other children may not want to play — they may prefer to build whatever they feel like building. Sometimes the symbol signs can just be used to stimulate discussion as everyone works on their creations. Also, you can always try the activity on another day — different days can bring different moods.

EXTENDING THE CONCEPT

art Using a large styrofoam meat tray and the other materials used for the spool community, build a giant ship for the spool people.

math While the children use the spools in their block play, ask them if they'd like to line up the spools from shortest to tallest, or fattest to thinnest.

dramatic play If you can get a toy sewing machine, or a real one which is broken (being sure though, to remove unsafe parts) set up a tailor's shop. Even if you can't get a sewing machine, ABC School Supply Inc. (address in Resources section) supplies a sewing basket kit. Or, if you can get plastic needles, put your own kits together. A fabric store may be able to donate old patterns and pattern books for the children's use. These will also help create a print-rich environment. If you can, provide a telephone, measuring tape or rulers for measuring, buttons, spools, a mirror, and fabric scraps. If you have enough fabric, wrap it around a cardboard cylinder to simulate a bolster of cloth. Provide a table for the children to work on, as well as a counter for taking customer orders. Make signs advertising specials. Ask the children what the tailor's shop should be called. Talk about how clothes are made.

LITERATURE

*Hest, Amy, *The Purple Coat*, Macmillan, 1986
*Blood, Charles, *The Goat In The Rug*, Parents' Magazine Press, 1976
*Hoban, Tana, *Count And See*, Macmillan, 1972

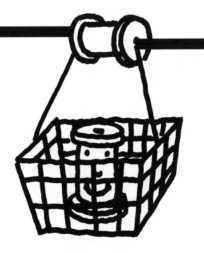

A-rumblin',

A-tumblin',

here it comes,

a naughty cylinder

on the run.

THEME: cylinders

A few weeks before you plan on implementing this theme, begin collecting cardboard tubes such as toilet paper rolls, paper towel rolls, tin foil rolls, wax paper rolls, and so forth. If you're a teacher, you can also ask parents to bring their rolls to school, and if you're a parent, perhaps neighbors will save their rolls for you. The larger a collection you have, with the greater range in size and diameter, the more interesting the activities will be.

INTRODUCTORY ACTIVITIES

Attention Grabber

Ahead of time, cover a toilet paper roll with interesting contact paper. Another option is to use realistic dinosaur, truck, or animal stickers to decorate the cylinder. Find your quiet spot away from where the activities are set up, and hide the cylinder behind your back. As the children approach, say: "I have something interesting behind my back, and I wonder if you can guess what it is." Give them clues until all the children arrive, and then pass it around to them. Tell the kids it's called a cylinder. For young children, say: "Let's tap that word on our noses," "Let's blink that word" and so forth, until the word is reinforced.

INTRODUCTORY DISCUSSION

objective   Introduce the theme to children; facilitate language development; develop cognition by memorizing words and identifying shapes.

materials   Cylinder rhyme
Open space

directions   Ahead of time, cut out a circle, square and triangle from construction paper. Together with the children, name the shapes. Then hold up the cylinder from the Attention Grabber activity, and roll it along the floor. Mention again that this is called a cylinder. Read the rhyme to the kids a few times, and then have them sit in a circle, several feet away from each other. Invite each child to roll the cylinder to the next child as the group recites the rhyme. When the cylinder has made it around the complete circle, ask children to guess what you'll be working with the next few days.

MUSIC/MOVEMENT
Cylinder Song

objective   Facilitate gross motor exercise; help children feel good about singing; develop cognition through memorization of words in the song; develop reading skills.

materials   Open space
Large piece of butcher paper
Marker

To the tune of Five Little Ducks Went Out To Play:
Cylinder, cylinder straight and tall,
Cylinder, cylinder fat and small,
Cylinder, cylinder there you lay,
Tumble over and roll away!

And: I can tumble and roll, but here's my strange riddle:
when I'm perfectly still you can climb through my middle.
What am I?

preparation   Make large picture charts for the above song and riddle.

directions   Hang the charts up where all the children will be able to see them. Go over the words and pictures with them, having them guess the meaning of as many pictures as possible. Sing the song and do the movements. For "Cylinder, cylinder straight and tall," stand on tiptoes with arms stretched as high as possible. For "Cylinder, cylinder fat and small," hunch down and make a hollow with your arms. For "Cylinder, cylinder there you lay," lie down on the ground. For "Tumble over and roll away," roll over and over. Here is the finger play for the riddle: For "I can tumble and roll," roll your index fingers around each other. "But here's my strange riddle": shake one pointer finger in an "I'm telling you" gesture. For "when I'm perfectly still," make a circle with your thumb and index finger. For "you can climb through my middle," use two fingers from your other hand, have them walk up to the circle and climb through it.

ACTIVITY CENTERS

ART:
Cylinder Prints

objective   Develop hand-eye coordination; facilitate experimentation with colors; facilitate experimentation with unusual painting utensils.

materials   Shallow containers
Cylinders with broad rims
   that vary as much as possible
   in diameter, from very
   small cylinders to very large ones.
Paint
Paper

preparation   Spread newspaper or a tablecloth out on the work surface. Mix red, green and blue paint and put each in a container. Spread the cylinders out on the table. If you're short of cylinders, and need to save most of them for the other activities, wrap tagboard around and staple it to make cylinders.

directions   Encourage the children to experiment with dipping the cylinders in paint, and making prints with them. If appropriate, comment on how there are rings within rings, and rings overlapping rings. Are there overlapping rings where two colors have made a new color?

ART:
Cylinder City

objective   Facilitate decision making; develop fine motor skills; facilitate creative expression.

materials   Fabric
Cylinders that vary in height and diameter
Toothpicks
Paper
Paper cups

Small boxes
Wooden blocks
Spools
Glue
Glue brushes
Large piece of tag board
Scissors
Markers
Pictures or posters of round buildings if possible

preparation Pin up your posters or pictures near your work area. Spread newspaper or a tablecloth over your work surface, and put the tag board down on it. (If you're a parent, and don't have tag board readily available, it can be purchased at school supply stores or craft stores.) Draw a few roads on the tag board, decorate one cylinder building either by coloring it or gluing materials onto it, and glue the building onto the tagboard to begin the city. Make flags with the fabric, and glue them onto toothpicks whose sharp ends have been snipped off. Also have available some flags and prepared toothpicks that have not been glued together for children who want to do that step themselves. Spread all materials out on the tag board.

directions Point out to the children the buildings in the pictures. Ask them what they see on the table, and what they could do with them. If your children are like mine, you'll see a cylinder city grow before your eyes. If, however, the children find something more interesting to do with the materials, encourage and support them.

SOCIAL STUDIES: Cylinder Community - continued from previous activity

objective Help children identify key buildings common to almost every community; initiate thinking about the functions of these community buildings; promote cooperative decision making; develop all components of language: speaking, listening, writing and reading skills.

materials Posters or pictures of community buildings such as the hospital, post office, school, police station, fire department, and so forth.
Popsicle sticks
Index cards
Putty or modeling clay
Markers
Glue
Sticky labels

preparation The purpose of this activity is to provide a variety of miniature signs, and to use them to name each building in the cylinder city. A stand-up sign can easily be made by gluing a piece of index card onto a popsicle stick. The name of the building can be written onto the sign, and the stick can be put into the putty so that it stands up. Cut different sign shapes out of the sticky labels unless you're working with older children who will want to cut out their own. Label and decorate one sign, and stick it onto a building. If you can't find the poster you need, make one yourself by cutting out photographs of buildings from magazines and gluing them onto butcher paper, or use the sample in the appendix to draw your own poster.

directions Look at the community buildings in the posters and pictures, and ask the children what they think each building is. After all the buildings have been identified, pick one, and ask: "Which building in our cylinder city should be the post office (or hospital or fire house) do you think?" If there is more than one choice, let there be two (or however many) post offices/hospitals/fire houses. Ask: "How will we know that that's the post office?" Facilitate a discussion about the signs on each building in the picture/s. Help the children listen to each other without interrupting. Ask them if they would like to make signs for the buildings in the cylinder city. Take story dictation from young preschoolers, and encourage older children to write the names of their own signs. Lead the discussion towards what the workers in each building do.

DRAMATIC PLAY:
Life In The Cylinder City

objective Facilitate the opportunity to act out real-life community scenarios; develop conversational skills; develop vocabulary.

materials Cylinder city
Toy people (Fisher Price people work well)
Toy vehicles — as many different kinds as possible: fire trucks, ambulances, school buses, trucks, cars etc.

preparation Put the toy people and vehicles in the cylinder city.

directions   Let the children explore and play. Try to achieve a balance between letting them engage in their own verbal interactions on the one hand, and on the other, asking questions to stimulate language development. Engaging in dramatic play with children can be very fun and satisfying for everyone, but allow plenty of time for the children to play by themselves, too.

SENSORY:
Cylinders And Styrofoam

objective   Facilitate sensory exploration of styrofoam and cylinders.

materials   Styrofoam packing — small, loose pieces
Containers
Cylinders
Sensory table or tubs

preparation   Place cylinders, styrofoam and containers in your sensory table or tubs.

directions   Stand back and let the children pour the styrofoam pieces through the cylinders, and to explore the materials in other ways.

GROSS MOTOR:
Tunnel Time

objective   Facilitate gross motor development.

materials   A tunnel of any kind   Gym mats
Ladder   Balance beam
Small trampoline   Optional: Climber

preparation   If you have access to gross motor equipment, arrange it all into an obstacle course and incorporate the tunnel. If you only have a tunnel, place it in front of an activity such that the children must climb through the tunnel to get to the activity.

directions   Once you've arranged an obstacle course, supervise closely.

SCIENCE/SENSORY:
Cylinder Sounds

objective   Facilitate experimentation with sounds produced from cylinders of varying lengths and diameters.

materials   Cylinders — as large a variety in terms of length and diameter as possible.
Tape recorder and tape
Activity sign (described below)

preparation   Lay cylinders out on a table or on the floor. Have your tape recorder nearby. Make a picture activity sign that says, "Would you like to make noises through the cylinders? Do they make different sounds?" and put it near the cylinders.

directions   Pick a cylinder up, and make a noise through it. Pick up another, very different one. Say: "I wonder if this cylinder will make

the same sound or a different one?" Encourage the children to experiment with making noises through the different cylinders, and to verbalize their findings. Suggest that they record their sounds, and let them press the necessary buttons. Play the sounds back to them, and discuss what you all hear. Do the children remember which cylinder made which sound?

MATH:
Cylinder Surprise

objective   Facilitate rational counting; develop all four components of language: speaking skills, listening skills, reading and writing skills.

materials   Cylinders which are as broad in diameter as possible
Construction paper
Four different colors of contact paper or paint.
Small pom poms (available at craft stores)
Small beads
Seeds
Beans
Double-sided tape
Tagboard
Glue
Pens

preparation   In this activity you're going to stick small items onto a circle which will be covered by a cylinder. The children pick up the cylinder and count the items they find underneath. There are two ways to make this project, depending on how much time you have. If you want it to be a simple counting exercise, cut out a tagboard strip on which four cylinders of diverse diameters can be placed. Trace around each cylinder. Stick double-sided tape on each circle you traced, making sure the tape extends beyond the edges, so that the cylinders will stick onto the tagboard. On each circle, stick a different number of each of the following: pom poms, beans, beads and seeds. The number should depend on how high your kids count. Then place each cylinder back over

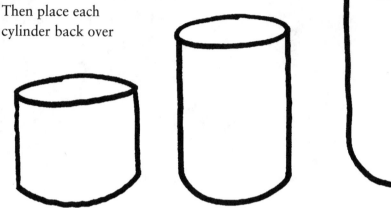

its circle. Make two sets of this game. If you have time to make this activity a color matching game too, then follow these additional instructions: Either paint four cylinders four different colors, or wrap them in four different colors of construction paper or contact. (Using contact paper is the easiest, but if you paint them, a fast way to do it is to quickly roll them in containers of paint.) On four pieces of construction or contact paper which match the cylinders in color, trace one end of each cylinder onto its matching color of paper. Cut out the circles you've traced. Using glue or double-sided tape, attach your four circles onto a strip of tagboard that accommodates them all. Lay strips of double-sided tape on each circle, making sure that the tape extends beyond the edges of each circle. This is so that the cylinder which goes on top of it will stick to the circle. Onto each circle, stick a varying number of each item: on one, stick pom poms; on another, stick on beads; on another, place seeds; and on the last, stick on beans. For kindergartners and older children, stick down amounts of teens and twenties in rows. Over these round patches, stick down the cylinder which matches in color. If you have time, you may want to wrap double-sided tape around the edges of each cylinder. Make two sets. Place each set opposite the other at a two-person work table. Near it, place a picture activity sign that says, "Would you like to count the surprises under the cylinders?" Place photocopies of writing sheets that ask, "How many (objects) under the cylinders?" at each place, and supply pens.

directions   For 3's and young 4's, speaking and listening skills take place when they talk to the child opposite them who is also involved in the same project. This is the beauty of two-person work stations: so often children verbally engage whoever is closest about what they're doing and discovering. Also, 3's and young 4's may not use the writing sheets for the specified purpose, but that's fine. They'll usually draw their own pictures, letters, or shapes on the writing sheets and in this way, will participate in reading and writing experiences. If you see two children who are not communicating with each other, or only one person at the table, you can approach the table yourself, and ask her/him/them about their discoveries.

MATH:
Cylinder Match

objective Facilitate matching exercise; promote self-esteem through sense of autonomy at one-person work table.

materials
Large piece of butcher paper
Cylinders as diverse in diameter as possible
Marker
Sign
Tub for cylinders

preparation Trace each cylinder end in thick, bold marker across the butcher paper. Place the cylinders in the tub, and put it nearby. Draw one stick figure, and the words "One person may be here." Lower down, write: "Would you like to match the cylinders?" For more advanced children, you can make this more difficult by having several cylinder outlines that are the same size, but are differentiated in some other way. For example, you could glue glitter on the outside of one cylinder, and glitter on its corresponding outline. Use color, fabric, yarn, or symbols cut out of construction paper for other creative ways of making the activity more challenging for older children.

directions Stand back and watch your children work!

LANGUAGE:
Tunnel Books

objective Develop all components of language: speaking and listening skills; reading and writing skills; develop fine motor skills.

materials
Toilet paper rolls	Magazines
Hole punch	Stapler
Sturdy, pale paper	Glue, glue brushes or glue sticks
Scissors; children's and adult's	Markers
Yarn or string	Glitter

preparation In this activity you're going to make a book that hides pictures under flaps. The flaps will be folded out of the first, third, fifth pages, and the pictures will be glued onto the second, fourth, and sixth pages underneath. You'll attach a "tunnel" or cardboard toilet paper roll to the book, and children look through the tunnel as they lift up the flap. Punch a hole near the edge of each toilet paper roll. Make blank books by folding over three same-sized pieces of pale paper, and stapling them close to the edge of the fold. This should yield a six-page book. Make one for each child. The top of each book will be the folded, stapled side. Punch a hole with the hole punch in the top left hand corner of each book. Cut lengths of yarn or string about a foot long, and tie a length through the hole in each book. Decorate the toilet paper roll for your own sample tunnel book. You can either color it using markers, decorate it with stickers, or paint it with glue and then dip it in glitter. Have the children decorate their own "tunnels" the day before they make their books. After your toilet paper roll is decorated, and glue has had time to dry, attach the tunnel to your book by tying the yarn or string that's already attached to the book to the hole in the toilet paper roll. Give your sample tunnel book a title by writing on the cover: "What's At The End Of The Tunnel?" Put the end of the toilet roll over interesting pictures you find in magazines, trace around the pictures, and cut them out. If you don't have time to trace and cut round pictures, then just cut out any shape so long as they fit on the book pages. Fold half of the first page in your book so that the lower half is a flap. Glue one of your pictures onto the second page, underneath the flap of the first page. Finish your book by using the rest of the pages in the same way: a flap page, a picture page, a flap page, a picture page and so forth. On each flap page, write a riddle for each picture, using simpler riddles for 3's and young 4's. (e.g. "I have four wheels and people go places in me. What am I?") Use more abstract riddles, which focus on function, for kindergartners. (e.g. "You'll find me in the sky, and I make things grow. What am I?" or "I'm sweet and people use me to bake treats. What am I?") Spread out on a table the blank tunnel books, pre-cut pictures, and glue sticks. If you're working with 5's and over, your kids may want to cut out and prepare all their own materials, including their own blank tunnel books.

directions Read your book to the children. Facilitate the development of speaking and listening skills by having the children take turns to come up to the book, look through the attached tunnel, guess, and then say, what the picture shows. When you finish reading the book, show the children the materials on the table, and ask them what they could do with them. After the children have decorated their own toilet paper rolls for tunnels, and when they're ready to make their books, develop reading and writing skills by taking story dictation from younger children, or, with older kids, writing out their words to be copied. Read the books back to the children if you like, or have the children read them back to you. Place the book you made, and if they're willing, some of the children's, on the children's book shelf for them to read themselves, later. There are a lot of fun things to do with these books. One child can look through her/his tunnel, describe one part of the picture, and then challenge a friend to find the same part. Children can also dictate descriptions of what they see through their tunnels.

EXTENDING THE CONCEPT

art/math   Have the children paint cylinders of varying lengths and afterwards, offer them the opportunity to roll the cylinders across paper. Examine the tracks when the cylinder pictures are dry. Which cylinder made which track?

math   Have a one-person work table with cylinders of varying sizes. Nearby, put up a picture sign that says: "Would you like to line up the cylinders from tallest to shortest?"

language/ cognitive   When the cylinder community is built, play an "I spy" game. Say, "I'm looking at the cylinder building where people will buy stamps." After the children guess which building you mean, encourage them to give you hints so you can guess the answer.

LITERATURE

*Hoban, Tana, *Over, Under And Through,* Macmillan, 1973
*Hoban, Tana, *Circles, Triangles And Squares,* Macmillan, 1974
*Hoban, Tana, *Shadows And Reflections,* Greenwillow, 1990
*Gibbons, Gail, *Tunnels,* Holiday House, 1984
*Sauvain, Philip, *How We Build Tunnels,* Garrett Educational Corporation, 1990

Button shower,

pitter patter,

small and round,

they clitter clatter.

THEME: buttons

Buttons are a lot of fun to examine and sort through, and a large collection lends itself to many natural math activities. If you don't have a collection, Lakeshore Learning Materials (address in appendix) has a button collection in their catalog. If you're going to start your own collection, visit a fabric store. They might have some old, unsold buttons in an "odds and ends" box which they'd be willing to give you. Tell them why you want the buttons; sometimes when people know you want materials for children, they're more willing to help.

INTRODUCTORY ACTIVITIES

Attention Grabber

Take an interesting-looking box or tin, and put some buttons inside it. As the children approach, shake the box or tin, and ask them if they can guess what you have inside. Give them hints until all the children arrive, and then let them examine your button container.

43

INTRODUCTORY DISCUSSION

objective Introduce the activity to children; facilitate listening and speaking skills.

materials Button rhyme

directions Read the rhyme to the children. "Accidentally" spill some of the buttons from your container. With the children, look at where the buttons landed. Which button bounced farthest away from the tin? Which is the biggest button? Which one is the smallest? Did the buttons make a sound when they landed on the floor? Ask the children if they've ever spilled anything when they were trying to open a container. Pick up the buttons together and look around at what everyone's wearing. Ask the children who's wearing buttons today.

MUSIC/MOVEMENT:
Button Song

objective Develop cognition by identifying parts of clothing; facilitate gross motor development; help children feel good about their singing voices.

materials Open space
To the tune of Here We Go 'Round The Mulberry Bush sing:
This is the way we button our shirts,
button our shirts, button our shirts,
this is the way we button our shirts,
all on a (name of day) morning.

directions Pretend to button a shirt as you sing the song. After this verse, ask the children what other pieces of clothing can be buttoned, and sing additional verses of the song, using their suggestions.

ACTIVITY CENTERS ART:
Paper Bag Puppets

objective Continue development of cognition by identifying parts of clothing; develop fine motor skills; develop self-esteem by providing decision-making opportunities; facilitate creative expression.

materials Large wiggly eyes (Available from Lakeshore supplies and virtually any craft or dime store)

No. 6 brown paper bags	Scissors
Yarn	Glue
Wallpaper	Markers
Construction paper	Buttons
Fabric	Fabric scraps

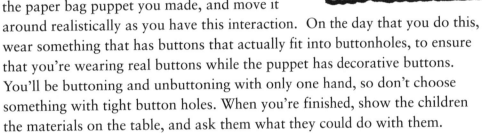

preparation   Cut out blank circles 4" in diameter. For kindergartners, you can let them do the following step themselves, but for preschoolers, glue one blank circle over the bottom of each bag, and cut across the area where the bottom lifts up. Cut out lengths of yarn for hair, and pants, shirts, and dresses from construction paper, wallpaper, and fabric. Kindergartners and older children may want to cut out their own clothes. Place all the materials on a table. Make a puppet yourself, using yarn for hair, wiggly eyes for eyes, and gluing buttons down the front of the shirt or dress.

directions   At the end of your morning's introductory activities, engage the children in dialogue using the puppet you made. Put your hand in the paper bag puppet you made, and move it around realistically as you have this interaction. On the day that you do this, wear something that has buttons that actually fit into buttonholes, to ensure that you're wearing real buttons while the puppet has decorative buttons. You'll be buttoning and unbuttoning with only one hand, so don't choose something with tight button holes. When you're finished, show the children the materials on the table, and ask them what they could do with them.

dialogue   You (to puppet): You know what, Oliver? I just noticed that we're both wearing buttons today. Come to think of it, I'm actually kind of hot. I think I'll open my sweater. (Unbutton sweater.)

Oliver: Yeah, good idea. I think I'll do the same. (Twist and bend puppet as if he's trying to unbutton his buttons.) Hey, wait a minute — they're not unbuttoning.

You (to children): Kids, do you think Oliver will be able to unbutton his buttons? Why not?

You (to Oliver): Oliver, some buttons are there for decoration, to make your clothes look pretty or interesting, and then other buttons really button. Which kind am I wearing, kids? And which kind is Oliver wearing?

You (to Oliver): Oliver, what color do you think my buttons are? (Have the puppet guess several wrong colors and then ask the kids to tell Oliver the answer.)

You (to Oliver): Oliver, are any kids wearing decoration buttons today? Do you see any?

(Have the puppet look for and talk about the children wearing decorative buttons.) Are any kids wearing buttons that button? (Have the puppet look for and talk about kids with real buttons. If you're working with older children, ask the them which kind they're wearing. If there are children who have no buttons, point out their zippers or snaps so they don't feel left out.)

ART:
Button Maracas

objective Develop self-esteem by providing children the opportunity to make their own musical instruments; develop fine motor skills.

materials Plastic soda bottles with caps or
frozen juice cans with lids
Glue
Tissue paper scraps
Buttons
Adult scissors

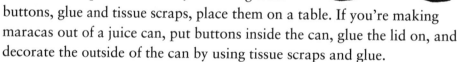

preparation Cut off the bottom end of each soda bottle so that it's 4" long, and cut off the top end so that it's 5" long. Put buttons inside, and fit the bottom into the top. If you like, you can put glue around the rim and sides to make it more secure. Decorate your maraca by gluing tissue scraps onto it, or, if you want the buttons to be visible, leave it undecorated. Cut out several more bottle tops and bottoms, and along with buttons, glue and tissue scraps, place them on a table. If you're making maracas out of a juice can, put buttons inside the can, glue the lid on, and decorate the outside of the can by using tissue scraps and glue.

directions During the introductory musical activity, use your maraca. When the song is finished, tell the children your instrument is called a maraca. With younger children say, "Let's tap that word with our feet. Let's pat that word on our heads. Let's shake that word with our maracas." Show the children the materials on the table, and ask them what they could do with them.

ART:
Button Boxes

objective Develop self-esteem by providing children with the opportunity to make a functional item they can take home and use; develop fine motor skills; facilitate creative expression.

materials Buttons
Small cardboard boxes with lids
Glue

Tempera
Glue brushes

preparation In order to have enough boxes, you'll probably have to start collecting them well ahead of time. On the morning of your activity, spread newspaper or an old tablecloth out on your work surface. Mix tempera paint with glue. You may want to have two or three different colors of glue. Place buttons and boxes on the table such that they are easily accessible to all children. The day before this activity, decorate your own box by gluing buttons around it. Find something interesting to keep in your box.

directions During the day's introductory activities, allow the kids to examine your button box and what you keep inside it. Show them the materials on the table, and ask them what they could do with them. It's a good idea to supply construction paper too, in case anyone wants to make button collages.

LANGUAGE:
Button Box Chart — continued from above activity

objective Develop speaking, listening and reading skills.

materials One large piece of butcher paper
Two markers of different colors
Tacks or masking tape

preparation Pin the blank chart up on the wall near the button box art project.

directions As the children work on their button boxes, ask them: "What are you going to use your button box for?" or "What are you going to keep in your button box?" Write down the children's answers using printscript or D'Nealian rather than cursive, and alternate the marker colors for each sentence. Use quotation marks, and write each child's name after his/her answer. Read the chart back to them when it's finished.

LANGUAGE:
Sook And The Lost Button

objective Develop listening and speaking skills; facilitate creative use of language.

materials Flannel board story below
"Two people may be here" sign
Flannel board pieces on pages 226, 227.

preparation Put your flannel board up at a table which will accommodate two children only. In a visible spot, put up the sign.

directions Tell the children the flannel board story, and then leave the board and the pieces out so that they can retell the story to each other, as well as make up new stories. When you make Sook's coat, glue or sew two buttons onto the flannel shape and glue or sew the third button onto a piece of velcro. Then glue or sew the matching piece of velcro onto Sook's coat, where the third button should be. This will make the third button detachable. To make the long grass, cut strips like a fringe into a piece of green flannel. To begin, attach the third button, and put the grass piece, Sook and her coat on the flannel board.

story   Once upon a time there was a woman whose name was Sook. Sook had a favorite coat, and it was her favorite coat because on it there were three beautiful, shiny buttons. [You can say to the kids: "Let's count and see if there are three."] Every day, Sook went walking out in the long, long grass. [Move Sook along flannel board as if she's walking. Without the children noticing, pull off the third button.] And every day she wore her favorite coat when she went on her walk.

But one day, when she got home from her walk, she noticed that one of her beautiful buttons was missing. "Oh, oh, oh," she said sadly, "One of the beautiful buttons from my beautiful coat is gone. It must have come off and fallen on the ground. I better go back and look for it in the long, long grass." So she went back outside, and pretty soon she met a donkey. [Put donkey on the flannel board.] And Sook said to the donkey: "Donkey, I've lost a beautiful button from my beautiful coat. Have you seen it in the long, long grass?" Donkey happened to be chewing a mouthful of grass just then, so she felt around with her tongue through all the grass in her mouth and her mouth went mrraow mrraow up and down and down and up and finally she said, "Nope. Can't say that I have." And she went off in the long, long grass looking for juicier grass to chew.

Sook was very sad, but she kept on looking. And pretty soon she met Rabbit [put rabbit on flannel board] and she said, "Rabbit, I've lost a beautiful button from my beautiful coat. Have you seen it in the long, long grass?" Rabbit happened to be snuffling through the grass just then looking for dandelion stems which were his favorite thing to eat. And so his twitching nose snuffled and sniffed and sniffed and snuffled through all the grass and finally he said, "Nope. Can't say that I have." And he hopped off in the long, long grass because he smelled some dandelion stems.

Sook was very sad, but she kept on looking. Pretty soon she met Mouse. [Put mouse and hole on flannel board] Mouse happened to be gathering dead grass and using it to line her nest which was in a hole in the ground. And Sook said, "Mouse, I've lost a beautiful button from my beautiful coat. Have you seen it in the long, long grass?" So Mouse went down to her hole and went through all the dead grass in her nest, scrabbling and scraping and scraping and scrabbling and finally she came back up to where Sook was standing and said, "Nope. Can't say that I have." And she went off in the long, long grass to find more dead grass.

Sook was very sad, but she kept on looking. Pretty soon she met Caterpillar, [put caterpillar and button on flannel board] and she said: "Caterpillar, I've lost a beautiful button from my beautiful coat. Have you seen it in the long, long grass?" Well, Caterpillar was trundling through the grass looking for a good place to make a cocoon and he was trudging and tromping and tromping and trudging through the long, long grass when it just so happened he bumped into something round and small and shiny. And he called up to Sook and said, "Well, I don't know if it's what you're looking for, but I found something small and round and shiny." Can you guess what it was?

And Sook was so happy! She said, "Caterpillar, thank you ever so much for finding the beautiful button to my beautiful coat. I'm going home right now to sew it on. And if you're looking for a good place to make your cocoon, there's a nice bush right outside my house." So Sook spent the afternoon sewing her beautiful button back onto her beautiful coat, and Caterpillar spent the afternoon making a cocoon in the bush outside Sook's house. And many days later a beautiful butterfly crawled out of that cocoon, and spent the day flying over the long, long grass. [Put butterfly on flannel board.

LANGUAGE:
Button Badges

objective   Develop speaking skills.

materials   Sticky labels
Marker
Buttons

preparation   Glue a button on each sticky label. Write: "Ask me what I did with buttons today!" Leave some badges blank for children who want to write or dictate their own questions.

directions Put a button badge on yourself. When the children ask you about it, ask them if they would like badges for themselves.

LANGUAGE:
Button Books

objective Develop all components of language: reading and writing skills; speaking and listening skills.

materials

Construction paper	Markers	Glue
Buttons	Stapler	

preparation Make blank books by folding several sheets of paper over and stapling close to the fold. Fold every other page to make a flap out of that page. Glue a button of a different color on every unfolded page, underneath the flap page in front of it. For each button, write a color riddle, such as: "I'm a button the same color as a tomato." For kindergartners or older children, write riddles which are more abstract, and focus on function or location: "I'm a button the color of things that grow on every tree." After making your book, spread all materials out on a table. Kindergartners may want to fold and staple their own books.

directions At the end of one morning's introductory activities, read your button book to the children. If practical, let them take turns coming up to where you are, guessing the button's color, and lifting up the flap to reveal the button underneath. When the book is finished, show them the materials on the table, and ask them what they could do with them. Take story dictation from preschoolers, and encourage older children to write their own riddles. When they are finished, read the books back to young children, and encourage older children to read their books to you.

DRAMATIC PLAY:
Paper Bag Puppet Theater

objective Facilitate coordination of speech and movement; facilitate release of emotions; provide opportunity to entertain others; provide opportunity to fantasize and create.

materials Puppet theater
Paper puppets made in above art activity

preparation There are plenty of ways to make a puppet theater if you don't have a store-bought one. One simple option is to lay a small table down on its side, and let children work behind it. Another is to hang a blanket across a doorway. You can also hang a blanket over a broom pole, and lay it across the backs of two chairs. The most fun method by far though, is to obtain a big refrigerator box, and cut out an opening in it. With this method, the children can decorate the box ahead of time and put the name of their theater on it as well.

directions Lay the puppets out in a visible place near the puppet theater. If the children are hesitant about using it, put a puppet on your hand, go behind the theater, and say a few words with your character before withdrawing to let the children take over.

GROSS MOTOR:
Button Hunt

objective Facilitate gross motor development.

materials Buttons   Marker
Paper bags

preparation Hide buttons in places that will require the children to do the following: climb, crawl, squat, and stretch. Write each child's name on a bag.

directions For younger children, hide the buttons in a smaller area and provide them with clues if necessary. Praise the children as they find the buttons. Have the paper bags open and sitting on the ground. Let the children drop their buttons into the bags, but it's not advisable to let them carry the bags while they're climbing, crawling and searching.

MATH:
Button Counting Cans

objective   Facilitate rational counting; develop all components of language: reading and writing skills; listening and speaking skills.

materials   Buttons
Eight small coffee cans with plastic lids, or Blue Diamond
      Almond cans with plastic lids.
Construction or contact paper — four different colors
Double-sided tape or glue
Photocopies of writing sheets (described below)
Pens
Sign (described below)
Razor blade or exacto knife

preparation   You'll be making two sets of four counting cans each. Wrap each of the four cans in a different colored paper, either gluing the construction paper onto the can, attaching it with double-sided tape, or sticking contact paper onto it. Using a razor blade or exacto knife, cut a slot in each plastic lid, just big enough for buttons to be passed through. Put a varying number of buttons in each can. For older preschoolers and kindergartners, put amounts in the teens and twenties. Place four cans, writing sheets and a pen at each place, and arrange them so that two children will be working opposite each other. Near their workplace, put up a picture sign that says: "Would you like to count the buttons in the cans? What do you hear when you drop a button in a can?" To make the writing sheets, draw a picture of each can, and put a scribble of color on each one that corresponds with its actual color. Under each can, write: "How many buttons in the (color) can?" Draw some buttons above each word, and put a scribble of color next to each color word. You'll probably want to wait to add the color scribbles until after you've made your photocopies.

directions   If only one child is at the table, then ask him/her about what he/she is experiencing, and encourage the child to describe his/her discoveries.

MATH:
Button Patterns

objective   Facilitate experience with patterns; facilitate matching experience for young children; promote cooperation as children help each other look for buttons.

materials | Buttons | Marker |
| --- | --- |
| Tagboard | Glue brushes |
| Glue | Double-sided tape |

preparation   Cut out tagboard pieces which are about a foot across, and two inches down. Rule the tagboard off using a horizontal line, so that there are two levels; an upper and a lower. Then, using vertical lines from top to bottom, draw dividers about an inch or so away from each other, until the whole of each tagboard piece is divided off. Using buttons, glue a pattern across the upper row so that there is a button in each section. The children can recreate the pattern in the lower level of the tagboard by gluing each matching button onto the blank section directly below the upper row you've filled in. With older children, you can rule off the tagboard and glue on buttons such that the kids will simply finish the pattern that's already been started. Also, rule off tagboard pieces and leave them empty with no buttons so that the children can create their own patterns. Blank cards also provide another option for children who don't wish to participate in the patterning activity. Put the pattern cards, glue, glue brushes, and buttons on a table such that all materials are accessible to all children. If you like, put long strips of double-sided tape along the lower level so that the kids can just stick the buttons on without glue. Since the buttons are then removable, this has the advantage of allowing several children to use the same pattern card. If your kids are going to take their finished pattern cards home though, glue is more permanent.

directions   During introductory activities, pick out a pattern card, and say: "Look at these buttons on here. Let's see, there's a black one, and then a yellow one, and then a black one, and then a yellow one — which color button do you think I should put on next for this pattern?" Show them the materials on the activity table. It's exciting to watch the children help each other look for the particular buttons they need to complete their button matches or patterns.

SCIENCE/SENSORY:
Button Shake

objective   Facilitate scientific exploration of the connection between number of objects and noise generated; develop sense of hearing.

materials   Four tins or coffee cans with lids
Buttons
Sign (described below)
Glue

preparation   Put just a few buttons in one tin or can and seal the lid. Put considerably more in the next container, and repeat this with the next two tins or cans in such a way that each has a graduated amount of buttons. Seal all lids with glue. Nearby, place a picture sign that says: "What do you hear when you shake the cans? Which can has the most buttons? How do you know?"

directions   If the children ask what the sign says, read it to them, or help them interpret/read it. As the kids explore the materials, ask them about their findings. Ask them about the weight of the cans. Is that another clue about how many buttons the can has?

SCIENCE/SENSORY:
Button Drop

objective   Facilitate experimentation with different surfaces and how they affect sound; develop sense of hearing.

materials   Cookie sheet
Piece of a towel, or a washcloth
Paper towel
4 Styrofoam trays
Piece of cardboard
Disposable aluminum pan
Glue
Container with buttons
Sign (described below)
Sensory table or tubs

preparation   Glue the towel fabric onto the bottom of one Styrofoam tray. Do the same with the paper towel and cardboard. Leave one styrofoam tray empty so that the kids can hear what it sounds like when buttons are poured on a styrofoam surface. Place the surfaces including the aluminum tray and cookie sheet, in tubs or in the sensory table. Place a container of buttons in the tub/s also. Nearby, attach a picture sign that says: "What do you hear when you pour the buttons?"

directions   Encourage the children to describe their findings. Ask them if the sound is different when they pour the buttons low down to the trays, or high up from the trays. Ask them if the sound is different when they pour slowly, compared to when they pour quickly.

SOCIAL STUDIES:
Class Or Family Button Collection

objective   Promote collective effort; show that sometimes collective effort is more effective than individual effort; develop speaking skills.

materials   Large plastic jar with lid
Large piece of butcher paper
2 differently colored markers

preparation Pin up the butcher paper in the spot where you hold your introductory activities. Have the empty jar nearby.

directions Ask the children if they would like to start a class/family button collection. Ask them: "Who could help us collect buttons?" Using alternate colors of marker, write down their answers on the chart. Also, ask them: "Where could we look for buttons?" and: "Where will we put the buttons we collect?" Read the chart back to them. If you're a teacher, ask the children if a note should be written asking parents to help with the collection. Take the children's dictation for the note, photocopy it, and have the children give the notes to their parents. If you're a parent, make the same kind of note in the same way for neighbors or extended family members. As the buttons start to fill up the jar, ask the children whether they would have such a big collection if only one person was looking for buttons. How did it help to have everyone collect buttons?

EXTENDING THE CONCEPT

math/science Put the jar with the collection of buttons on a small table, with pens and small sheets of paper. Nearby, place a sign that says: "Would you like to predict how many buttons are in the jar?" Talk to the children about what "predict" means, and what a prediction is. After everyone has made a prediction, count all the buttons together.

language/ math One morning, make a charted graph of how many buttons each child is wearing, and what color they are. As well as numerals and colors, write the words for each number and color.

fine motor "Dressy Bessy" dolls are terrific for helping young children develop buttoning, zipping, snapping and tying skills.

music Let the children use their maracas while listening to Ella Jenkins' record album, *Play Your Instruments And Make A Pretty Sound.*

LITERATURE

*Freeman, Don, *Corduroy*, The Viking Press, 1968
*Hoyt-Goldsmith, *The Totem Pole*, Holiday House, 1990
The Totem Pole is too wordy to read in its entirety, but it has wonderful photographs of a beautiful button blanket. Talk the children through it, or

discuss the photographs. This is a good book to read on the day when your paper puppet tells her/his story about the difference between buttons that button, and buttons that are just decoration.

Reid, Margaret S., *The Button Box*, Dutton Children's Books 1990

Lohf, Sabine, *Things I Can Make With Buttons*, Chronicle Books, 1989 (Excellent picture book)

Teaching From
NATURE

Sun

Rocks

Insects &

Spiders

Water

Sheening, shining
glints and dazzles,
hotly, brightly
glimmers,
dapples.

THEME: sun

To get the most out of this unit, it's really best to do it during hot weather. If you have a sunny class room or living room, it'll be easy to point out or talk about the patches of sunlight you see inside. Also, when you're out in your school yard or garden, you can ask the children where they see the sunlight on the tree leaves, and how those leaves differ in color from the shaded ones. Magazine pictures are mentioned in this unit. If you can, ask neighbors, relatives, or parents to help you collect old magazines. Nature, food, and wildlife publications are always useful to have on hand.

INTRODUCTORY ACTIVITIES

ATTENTION GRABBER

Find a photograph or drawing of the sun in a magazine and glue it inside a card made out of construction paper. Make the outside of the card interesting by putting star stickers on it. As the children gather, tell them you have a picture of a star that they have seen before, and that you wonder if they can guess which one it is. Give them hints like: "It's a star that makes us warm." When everyone's had a guess or made a comment, pass the card around for them to look at. Ask if they're surprised to find out that the sun is a star.

INTRODUCTORY DISCUSSION

objective   Introduce the theme; develop speaking and listening skills.

materials   The sun rhyme and any pictures or drawings of the sun that you've been able to obtain, especially a simulated drawing of the sun and other stars in space.

directions   Read the sun rhyme to the children and show them the illustrations. Ask them: "What is this poem talking about, do you think?" "Have you ever seen the sun suddenly come out from behind a cloud?" "Did you see any sun today?" Describe what each word means if the children don't know. You can see a sheen or a glint when sun shines on metal. Something that dazzles is something very, very bright. The sun glimmers when leaves wave back and forth in front of sunlight, and the sun hides and comes back quickly, and hides and comes back quickly, over and over again. All you see then is a glimmer. Sunlight dapples on water or on the ground through leaves. In general, looking up you see glimmers, looking down you see dapples. Some of your magazine pictures may help in your explanations. Show the children the picture of the sun in space and refer to the sun as a star. Compare the size of the earth to the size of the sun.

MUSIC/MOVEMENT:
Sun Song

objective   Develop cognition through memorization of words; encourage children to sing; reinforce the concept that the sun is a star.

materials   To the tune of Twinkle, twinkle little star:

Sunny, sunny giant star,
Shining brightly from afar
Up above our world so high,
Sending rays down from the sky,
Sunny, sunny giant star,
Shining brightly from afar

directions   Tell the children you are all going to pretend to be the sun. Ask the children if they think you can all pretend to be something that hot and that huge. If you like, sing "Twinkle, twinkle little star" first. For "Sunny, sunny giant star," try to make your bodies as big, round, and giant as possible. For "shining brightly from afar," reach your arms out like rays, and twinkle (wiggle) your fingers. For "up above the world so high," put your hands over your eyes and pretend to peer down at the earth. For "sending rays down from the sky," twinkle your fingers and point them down at the ground.

ACTIVITY CENTERS

ART/SCIENCE:
Sun Collage

objective   Facilitate creative expression and development of fine motor skills; develop social and emotional skills through cooperation and team work; facilitate observation of the effects of light on different kinds of paper, tin, and plastic.

materials   A giant sun shape cut out of butcher or chart paper
Collage scraps of tin foil, colored plastic paper (acetates),
plain paper, wax paper, brown lunch bag paper, plastic bag scraps.
Glitter or sparkly sequins
Glue
Glue brushes

preparation   Save gold foil paper from candy bars, or other interesting wrappers, and ask family, neighbors, or parents to do the same. If you have difficulty gathering shiny, acetate papers, try asking photocopying services or graphic design studios for donations of interesting, spare paper. Be sure to tell them that it's for a project with young children. If you work for a non-profit organization, you could mention that fact also. At our school, we've often thanked businesses in our newsletters, and encouraged parents to patronize those businesses. Some organizations are very willing to donate materials in return for this kind of free advertising. When you have your materials, spread newspaper out on a table, and arrange all materials on the work surface such that they will be easily accessible to the children. Include blank pieces of construction paper for kids who want to make an individual picture of another kind. Save one small (one square inch or so) sample of each kind of paper for the activity below.

directions   Encourage the children to glue the paper and plastic scraps onto the sun shape. Let them know it's O.K. to scrunch the paper up if they'd like to. When the sun collage is dry, either stay indoors and hold it up to sunshine, or, as a family or class, carry it outside together on a sunny day. Which papers or plastics reflect the sunlight? Which ones don't? See the activity below for extending this project.

MATH:
Paper Reflection Chart

objective   Facilitate classifying experience; facilitate rational counting.

materials   Sun collage from art activity above
Paper scraps held back from activity
Large piece of chart or butcher paper
Bold marker
Glue, tape or glue sticks

preparation   Using the marker, divide the chart into two columns. Head each column by material that reflects sunlight, and material that doesn't. Tape or pin this chart to a wall, for use after your observation of the papers on the sun collage.

directions   After the children have observed the reflective capabilities of each kind of paper on the collage, invite them to make a chart. Let the children take turns holding a sample of each paper type to sunlight, and then gluing it under the appropriate column, reflective or non-reflective. For older children, make writing sheets based on the chart column headings, but add the words: "How many?" Encourage the kids to count how many of kinds of paper did reflect sunlight and how many didn't, and to write the number of each on the writing sheet.

ART/SENSORY:
Hand Print Suns

objective   Provide sensory experience through hand painting; facilitate fun with art.

materials   Pieces of paper with a circle drawn on each; a circle which is about the size of a child's palm.
Two or three shades of yellow paint in pans large and shallow enough for kids to use for hand painting.

preparation   Spread newspaper and all materials on the table. Use white paint to lighten the shades of yellow. Taking one of the pieces of paper, make a sample yourself, first. Using your fingers to make the rays, and keeping your palm in the circle, move the paper around and make several hand prints so that the 'sun rays' extend around the entire circle.

directions   During introductory activities, show the kids your sun print, and show them the materials on the table. Ask them to guess how you made your sun print. When they approach the activity table, encourage them to put their hands in the paint. Encourage older 4's and kindergartners to write their own names on their pictures, as well as anything else they'd like to say about them. Put out some blank paper too, for kids who want to make different kinds of pictures.

MATH:
Sun Seriation

objective   Facilitate seriation activity; facilitate an understanding of ordinal numbers.

materials   Yellow construction paper
Tag board
A marker
A picture sign saying:
    "Would you like to sort the suns
    from biggest to smallest?"
Writing sheets (described below)
Pens
Stickers
Contact paper

preparation   If you can't find or make yellow tagboard, make all your suns white instead. Using a photocopier which reduces and enlarges, or by free hand drawing, make four or five suns of graduated sizes from the sample in the margin. For kindergartners and older children, make seven or eight, starting with a tiny one, and graduating in size to a very, very large one. If you have time, you can draw faces on the suns and cover them on both sides with contact paper to make them sturdier. If you don't have time to cut out the exact outline of each sun shape, just cut around them. Mix the suns up, and place them on a tray near an empty work surface, and then place the sign nearby. It can be fun to start off with a really huge sun that you've made from tagboard. For older kids, provide the writing sheet which helps teach the concept of ordinal numbers. To make it, photocopy several suns of different sizes from the collection you made above onto a single page. Have children color in the second and fourth suns (or any ordinals, based on the number of suns you fit on the page).

directions Encourage the children to approach the materials and explore them. Some children will ask you what the sign says. Invite them to interpret the symbols as well as they can while you read the words.

SCIENCE:
Plant Experiment

objective Facilitate the understanding that seeds need light to continue growing; develop positive self-esteem through independent, child-initiated experiment preparation; develop fine motor skills; develop powers of observation.

materials Small plastic cups
Tin trays
Small seeds (Bird seed, marigold, or zinnia seed is good.)
Sticky label paper
Markers
Potting soil
Spoons
A big box
Eye or medicine droppers
Small table

Butcher paper
Signs (described below)
Markers
Pens

preparation In this activity, you're going to use a box to create a dark environment in which to grow seeds, and you'll compare their progress with seeds grown in sunlight. Punch holes in the bottom of the plastic cups for drainage, and after seeds are planted, put the cups in the tin trays so that excess water is contained. You may want to cut the cups down by trimming several inches off the top edges. Cut off the flaps on the opening of the box. Cut a flap from one side and fold it back to make a door that will open and close. To make the flap easier for young children to open and close, cut a hole in the flap through which small hands can fit. Put the box on a table, opening side down, with the flap side accessible. Spread newspaper on the table, making sure that the table is near sunlight if possible. Have soil, spoons, cups, seeds, labels, and markers available on another near-by work surface. Make a picture sign that says, "Do seeds grow without sun? What happens if you put some seeds in a dark box, and some seeds in the sunlight?" Place this sign on the box, and another picture sign giving planting instructions, on the table. Pin up the blank butcher paper to use as an observation chart, and put out paper and pens on a nearby work surface.

directions During introductory activities, ask the children whether they think seeds will grow without sunlight. Let them know they can use the materials on the table to conduct a science experiment to find out. Encourage each child to put soil and seeds in two cups. Show them the labels and markers. In addition to making sure that each child's name is on his or her container, encourage the kids to label their plants in whatever ways they would like. Invite them to look in the box. Is there light in there? What will happen if we put one container of seeds in the box, and keep one out in the light? If no or few children want to put their seeds in the box, you can put yours in. Have eye or medicine droppers available for watering; by limiting the amount administered you avoid over-watering. Check on the plants and take dictation of

observations. (You will see some growth in the seeds in the box.) If some children dig up their seeds or drop their containers and replant their seeds, record these incidents to see if or how they affect the seeds. After both sets of seeds have sprouted and been given some time to grow, make a language chart of comparisons.

SENSORY: Reflections

objective Stimulate sense of sight; facilitate exploration with reflected light; develop self-esteem and sense of autonomy through one-person work station.

materials
A large appliance box
A flashlight
Aluminum foil
Piece of cardboard
A one-person work table

preparation In this activity, you're going to use a large box to create a dark environment in which the kids can explore light from a flashlight and reflected light from tin foil. Cut any flaps off the top of the box. Cut a large flap in the side of the box and fold it back to make a door, such that a child can sit at a table and comfortably put her/his torso inside. Wrap the aluminum foil around the cardboard, and place it on the table, inside the box. (If you would rather not use your own personal or family flashlight for fear of breakage, I've been able to find cheap flashlights for $2.00 or so, which I can let the kids use without worrying.) Place your flashlight on the table, in the box, and put a sign on the front. Draw one stick figure on it, and write: "One person may be here." During the morning's introductory activities, discuss this sign with the children, and what it means. Also shine the flashlight around the room, and ask the kids how the light from the flashlight differs from the light of the sun. Are they both as bright? Which one gives the most light? Which one can we turn on and off whenever we like? Show the children the batteries in the flashlight. If you have a small enough group, let them explore this facet of the flashlight.

directions At one point during free play, stick your head in the box yourself, shine the flashlight on the tin foil, and move the tin foil. Say: "Look what's happening!" (The reflected light will dance on the walls and roof of the box.) Or ask a child to shine the flashlight while you briefly move the tin foil. Younger children may not be as interested in the tin foil, but they'll enjoy using the flashlight.

NATURE/GROSS MOTOR:
Nature Walk

objective   Provide gross motor exercise; stimulate awareness of the sun as a source of heat and light; explore how sunlight is reflected.

materials   A piece of aluminum foil for each child
Cardboard (optional)

preparation   Before you go on your nature walk, talk to the children about how dangerous it is to stare at the sun. Tell the children that the sun is a very, very strong star which can hurt their eyes if they look at it for too long. Give each child a piece of tin foil. If you have time, you can wrap the tin foil around cardboard to make it sturdier. Ask the children what they think the tin foil will look like if the sun shines on it. Suggest to the children that on your walk, you look for other things that the sun makes shiny and sparkly, but talk about the dangers of picking up glass or metal.

directions   Go for a nature walk to see how much sun you can all see or feel. If the sun is out, notice what it does to the tin foil. If it's a hot day, feel different surfaces — cement, chain link fences, car hoods, and so forth, to see how warm, cold or hot they are. Compare standing in the shade to standing in the sun. Coming out into sunlight suddenly sometimes makes me sneeze, and I tell the children this and ask them if it ever happens to them. Ask the children to look up at the clouds. Is the sun hiding behind them? As you go on your walk, you'll have plenty of your own creative ideas and experiences to explore with the kids in regard to the sun and its light.

LANGUAGE/DRAMATIC PLAY:
The Sun And The Dinosaurs

objective   Stimulate the children to tell their own stories using the flannel board characters; develop

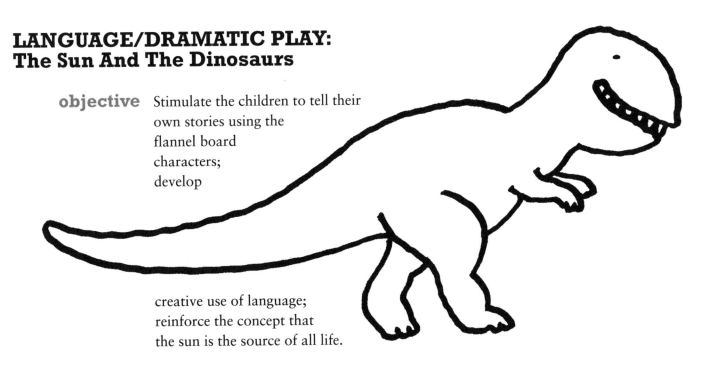

creative use of language; reinforce the concept that the sun is the source of all life.

materials Flannel board pieces on page 228
A "Two People May Be Here" sign

preparation Cut out flannel board pieces. Set up flannel board.

directions Tell the story below during your introductory activities, and then leave the flannel board and pieces out. Children can then retell the original tale, and make up their own stories from their imaginations, each child assuming the role of a particular character. The pieces of this flannel board story can be shapes only except for the sun, which is more effective with a face on it.

story [To begin, put the grass piece on the flannel board, and the sun high up, above it.] Once upon a time, long, long ago, before buildings, before computers, and even before people, there was nothing but jungle and dinosaurs. One day Tyrannosaurus [put Tyrannosaurus on the board] came roaring through the jungle and said, "I am Tyrannosaurus. I have very sharp teeth, and I am the fiercest and strongest in the jungle. I am Queen of the Jungle and I rule everything I see." and she let out a mighty roar.

Well, pretty soon Brontosaurus came along [put Brontosaurus on the board] and said, "I couldn't help overhearing what you said and you're wrong. *I* am the strongest and fiercest in the jungle.

I have the longest neck, and I am tall and strong. I am King of everyone in the jungle." Well Tyrannosaurus' stomach was quite full just then, so she decided to argue with Brontosaurus instead of eating him. [Move characters as if they're arguing.] They were just starting to fight about it: "You're not the fiercest — I am." "NO! I am — I'm the King." "No you're not!" "Yes I am!" and on and on, when who should come along but Stegosaurus.

[Put Stegosaurus on the board.] And Stegosauros said, "You're both wrong. I have sharp spikes on my tail and I lash it around. I am strong and fierce, and *I* am The Ruler of the Jungle." And she let out a mighty roar. [Move characters as if they're fighting.] Well, they were just starting to fight about it all over again: "Who asked you? You're not the fiercest!" "Well, I'm fiercer than both of you." "No you're not!" "You are not!" "Yes I am!" and so forth, when who should come along but Triceratops.

[Put Triceratops on the board.] You can probably guess what Triceratops said — that he was the fiercest and strongest because of the very sharp horn on his head, and that of course he was King of the Jungle. [Move characters as if they're arguing.] And you can just imagine the arguing then: "You're not fiercer than me!" "Yes I am — I'm much fiercer than you." "No you're not! That's ridiculous!" "I am too!" "No, I am." "No, I am." And so on and so on and so on. Well, they made so much racket that every dinosaur in the jungle must have heard them for miles. The Sun heard them, and came out from behind a cloud.

S/he [move sun as if it's speaking. Alternate the gender of the sun each time you tell the story] said, "Silence!!! I have something to say." And all the dinosaurs jumped in surprise, and were suddenly very, very quiet, and looked up at the sun meekly (although not for long, because it was bad for their eyes.) "Tyrannosaurus, Brontosaurus, Stegosaurus and Triceratops, if anyone is Queen of the Jungle, I am. I shine on everything, making it grow. I give you heat and light to live in. The plants that you eat grow because of me. I shone on you all when you were just little eggs, and I shone on you all when you were hatching out of those eggs. But I'm not interested in being Queen of the Jungle, and you have no reason to either. Would it make the plants juicier? Would it make the days warmer? Would it make the flowers smell sweeter? Would it make your eggs hatch faster? Would it make your babies stronger? No. Stop arguing about it. Know that I shine on all, I give heat and light to all, and go in peace." And all of a sudden, they all felt kind of silly and [move dinosaurs in different directions] they went off in different directions to find something good to eat (in Tyrannosaurus' case, another dinosaur.) And the sun laughed, and shone hot and bright all that long, sunny day.

SOCIAL STUDIES:
Weather Person

objective   Promote self-esteem through special helper job; facilitate observation skills by observing the weather; facilitate matching activity by matching a symbol with the weather.

materials   Tagboard
Markers
Double-sided tape
Yarn
Newspaper weather sections
(preferably the ones
in color)

preparation   Make a weather
board by writing the
words on a board and leaving a
space for a symbol. Using the art in the clip art section, make a card for each
kind of weather. Put double-sided tape on the space on the weather board
where the symbol card will be placed, and also, put double-sided tape on the
back of each symbol card. Place the weather board on the wall at the
children's eye level. Make a "Weather Person" badge and punch a hole about
an inch away from the edge on each side. String yarn through. This is the
official "Weather Person" badge that each child will wear when it's his/her
turn to be weather person.

directions   One morning during introductory activities,
show the children the weather board, the
symbols, and the "Weather Person" badge.
Read the words to them if appropriate. Ask
them who could be the weather person.
Almost certainly they will suggest
themselves, and you can brainstorm with the
kids to decide how everyone can have a turn
to be the weather person. The weather
person can look out the window, pick out the
symbol that best describes
the weather for the day, and
stick it on the weather
board. Ask the children who else
tells the weather. Do they ever see a
weather person on television? You
could also bring in the weather forecasts from the
newspaper for discussion and coloring. Pin some up on
the walls of the room.

EXTENDING THE CONCEPT

social studies If it's possible, ask the weather person at your local television station if you can bring the children for a visit, or alternatively, if s/he can visit your home or center and bring some of her/his weather forecasting tools and charts. Be sure to mention the age of your kids, and their comprehension level.

dramatic play If you'd like to extend the flannel board story, put out one of the tagboard suns from the sun seriation math activity and some toy dinosaurs and blocks, and let the children act out that story and new ones.

science/art Cut out medium or small sized circles, triangles, and squares from construction paper. Let the children staple their small shapes to larger pieces of construction paper, or, if they can be put in an out-of-the-way place, the kids can simply lay the shapes on without necessarily attaching them. Put the paper out on a window sill, or in an area exposed to sunlight, and after some time has passed, help the children remove their small shapes. Compare the areas of the larger piece that were covered by shapes to the areas that weren't. What did the sunlight do?

language After you plant your seeds for the darkness/sunlight science experiment, make a prediction chart by taking dictation of the kids' predictions.

LITERATURE

*McDermott, Gerald, *Arrow to the Sun*, Picture Puffin, 1991
Branley, Franklyn M., *The Sun - Our Nearest Star*, Thomas Y. Crowell, 1988
Branley, Franklyn M., *Sunshine Makes The Seasons*, Thomas Y. Crowell, 1985 (Older kids)
*Branley, Franklyn M., *What Makes Day And Night*, Thomas Y. Crowell, 1986 (Either use with older kids, or talk younger ones through it.)
Simon, Seymour, *The Sun*, William Morrow & Co., 1986 (Good picture book)
*Kandoian, Ellen, *Under The Sun*, Dodd, Mead & Co., 1987 (Good book for young kids)
Westberg Peters, Lisa, *The Sun, The Wind And The Rain*, Henry Holt & Co., 1988
You may need to talk the children through some of the more scientifically oriented books, but they'll probably still be interested.

Heave 'em, haul 'em hear 'em SPLUNK; craggy jaggy rocks are sunk.

THEME: rocks

About a week before this theme, let the children know you'll be studying rocks, and ask them to start gathering their own collection of rocks and stones to bring in the next week. It would be wonderful if you were able to provide all the kids with small boxes for this purpose. Cigar boxes are best, and tobacco and pipe stores will sometimes save these for parents and teachers. Another option is to implement this theme after Christmas and Chanukah so that gift boxes can be saved. The activities in this unit don't emphasize strongly the concept of hard and soft rocks, or names of the different kinds of rocks, because my experience with 3, 4, and even 5 and 6 year olds is that this information can be a little too sophisticated for them.

However, I have included some basic information below which would certainly be appropriate for introductory discussions. Also included is a hard/soft rock test that might be of interest to kindergartners, and which sometimes appeals to younger children, depending on the kids. This simple experiment will lay the foundation for the more detailed information they'll receive later in elementary school.

INTRODUCTORY ACTIVITIES

ATTENTION GRABBER

There are a couple of fun ways to generate interest in this theme. One is to go to a nature store or a Hearthsong branch, and buy a collection of semi-precious stones. My collection only cost a few dollars. You can put them in an interesting box or tin, shake it, invite the children to guess what's inside, and then let them examine the contents. Another method is to take an ordinary stone that will fit in your hand, and tell the kids that inside your hand you have something which may have been on the earth even before the dinosaurs thousands and thousands of years ago, and is very, very old. Show them your rock, and let their reaction lead into a discussion.

INTRODUCTORY DISCUSSION

objective
Facilitate understanding of where rocks come from; stimulate verbal expression; develop observational skills; generate interest in the theme.

materials
Pictures of volcanoes and flowing lava from magazines or books.
Pictures of rivers, lakes or oceans
Pictures of rocks
A metamorphic rock, like granite
An igneous rock, available from landscaping or construction companies
A sedimentary rock, such as limestone, flint, or shale
A container of gravel
Rock rhyme
A sealed plastic container with water and gravel inside

directions
If you're working with younger children, you may decide to introduce each kind of rock on separate days. There are three kinds of rocks:
Igneous rocks are made from lava.
Sedimentary rocks are created after erosion has reduced rocks to the small particles which form the sediment at the bottoms of rivers, lakes and oceans. Over time, the sediment is pressed and hardened into sedimentary rocks.
Metamorphic rocks are igneous and/or sedimentary rocks which are melted by heat and pressure under the earth's crust, and cool into rocks with a new form and shape.

Read the children the igneous rock rhyme below and pass around your igneous rock(s). Show children pictures of volcanoes and flowing lava and discuss them.

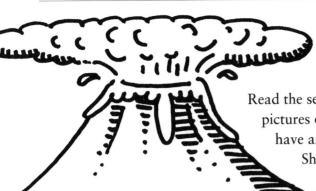

Igneous Rock

From erupting volcanoes lava runs;
that's where igneous rock comes from.

Read the sedimentary rock rhyme below, and then hold up the pictures of rivers, lakes and oceans. Pass any sedimentary rocks you have around for children to touch and hold.

Shake your container of water and gravel and ask the kids to notice what the gravel does. Introduce the word "sediment" and with young children, tap the word on parts of your body as you repeat it.

Place the container on an activity table for exploration.

Sedimentary Rock

The wind and water make big rocks break;
the particles sink in oceans and lakes.
They're pressed and hardened over time,
to make the sedimentary kind.

Read the metamorphic rock rhyme (below) to the children and pass around the granite or any other metamorphic rocks you have found. Ask the children to guess what you will be working with for the next few days.

Metamorphic Rock

Sedimentary and igneous rocks do meet,
under the earth with pressure and heat.
Pressure and heat make them melt and change,
into metamorphic rocks so strange.

MOVEMENT:
Rock Rhyme

objective   Develop cognitive skills through word memorization; develop large muscle groups.

materials   Rock rhyme on page 72, open space

directions   For "Heave 'em Haul 'em," pretend to haul a huge rock down a steep slope. Grunt and pant for realism. For "Hear 'em SPLUNK," pretend to heave your rock into water and stand back to avoid the splashes. For "craggy jaggy," make your hands, arms, and whole body as angular as possible. For "rocks are sunk," pretend to be a rock sinking slowly and heavily down to the bottom of a pond, and if you like, roll over when you get there.

MUSIC:
Rock Around

objective   Develop listening skills; develop hand-eye coordination; have fun!

materials   A rock that fits well into small hands
A tape recorder
Music (Bill Haley's Rock Around The Clock if you can!)

directions   Encourage everyone to sit in a circle. Tell the children that when the music is on, you're going to pretend the rock is hot lava. Turn the music on, and pretend yourself that the rock in your hand is so hot you can barely hold it. Turn the music off, and freeze into a rock. Tell the children that when the music stops, the lava instantly turns into rock, and then the person holding it turns into a rock too. After playing this game for a while, and if feasible, let the children take turns being the ones to turn the tape player on and off. They will tend to turn it off too frequently, but you can suggest that they wait a little while in between stops.

LANGUAGE:
Rock Collection Days

objective   Develop speaking and listening skills.

materials   The children's rock collection
Cigar boxes or other boxes

preparation   In advance of your "show and tell" rock collection days, ask the kids during introductory activities whether or not they'd like to start their own rock collections. Talk about how and where they could look for their rocks. If you like, make an activity out of decorating the collection boxes. With five or more very young children, I find it's too much stress on all of us to have everyone participate in a "show and tell" in the same sitting, because the kids have too much difficulty sitting still that long. If you have a large group of children, or very young ones, break up your group so that a small number of kids show their rock collections on different days. Let the children know ahead of time which day is their rock day, and if you're a teacher, you may want to remind parents. If there are children who have no rock collection, ask them if they would like to pick out some rocks to talk about from the collection you've been using for activities.

directions   Invite the children to show and talk about their rock collections to the other kids. Ask questions like "Do you have a favorite rock in your collection?", "Where did you find that one?" etc. Ask the other children if they have questions.

ACTIVITY CENTERS

GROSS MOTOR:
Rock Splunk

objective   Facilitate fun with rocks and water; develop large muscles.

materials   Very large rocks, or medium to small rocks, depending on where you'll be doing this project.
Water
A pool or tubs

preparation   This project depends on the weather. If it's a hot day, and the children can safely get wet, put a pool of water outside, and several very large rocks. If you need to do the project inside, you'll want to use smaller (probably much smaller!) rocks or stones, tubs of water, and lots of surrounding newspaper.

directions   Before this activity, discuss the importance of throwing the rocks/stones/pebbles <u>only</u> in water, and not at other people. Ask the kids what would happen if they threw them at each other. During the activity, encourage the kids to throw or drop the rocks in the water. Concentrate on what they see (splashes), feel (splashes), and hear (splashes!) If you're using very large rocks outside, have rules about where the waiting kids should stand while waiting their turn, to ensure that no one gets hurt. Masking tape lines can be useful to demarcate areas.

ART/SENSORY:
Sand And Rock Collages

objective Facilitate fine motor development; foster appreciation for objects of nature; facilitate creative constructing; provide sensory experience with a variety of natural materials; convey the concept that sand is broken-up rock.

materials

Gallon, quart and pint milk cartons
Sand
Stones
Leaves
Nut shells
Twigs
Seashells
Any other natural objects of interest
Large popsicle sticks or spatulas

preparation The above list of natural objects may seem intimidating, but believe it or not, I was able to collect most of what I needed in one quick trip around the school yard. Don't worry about gathering your collection — my experience is that the kids aren't picky, and find delight in some of the most ordinary objects. You may want to ask your extended family, neighbors and/or school/center parents to help you collect the milk cartons ahead of time. Cut all cartons lengthwise in half. Glue back together the top part which was peeled away to pour milk. Spread newspaper on the work surface, and arrange the cartons and nature objects such that they are easily accessible to all children. Wet the sand so that objects pushed into it will stay put, and place the sand in one big bowl or two, in the middle of the table. Make a sample collage yourself. You can make your sample by filling a carton with wet sand, packing it down, smoothing it, and pressing down into it whatever objects appeal to you.

directions During the introductory activities, show the kids your sand collage. Ask them where they think sand comes from, and tell them that rocks are broken down by water, wind, heat and cold. Tell them your sand used to be part of bigger rocks. If you're working with older children, put the wet sand in a large tub with a big spoon, so that they can take their own. For younger kids, you may have to help them take the sand out after they've chosen their collage carton.

ART:
Chalk Drawing

objective Develop fine motor skills; facilitate creative expression; provide kids with the opportunity to use different drawing tools; convey the concept that chalk is a soft rock.

| materials | Fat, colored chalk (Thin chalk breaks too easily) |

| preparation | Find a good spot outdoors which allows enough space for chalk drawing. (If it's raining, draw on dark paper.) |

| directions | Take the kids outside to make chalk drawings on the ground. As they do, tell them that chalk is a soft rock (pressed gypsum). When the children are finished, talk about their art. You may want to invite neighbor children or another class to come and see their art. |

SCIENCE:
Gravel Experiment

| objective | Promote the concept that water makes some things heavier and has a weight of its own; provide experience with measuring and comparing; provide exposure to the concept of equal and unequal weights and balances; develop fine motor skills; provide sensory experience with wet and dry gravel. |

| materials | Gravel (preferably gravel that's not artificially colored)
Small pitchers of water
Colanders
3 plastic tubs
Balancing scales
Two small scoops the same size (small plastic apple-sauce containers are perfect).
Picture sign saying: "What happens when you weigh wet gravel against dry gravel?" |

| preparation | If you have a large sensory table, you may want to conduct this project inside it. If you're using a table, spread plenty of newspaper on it. For each set of materials, set out the following: on one side of the balancing scales, put the dry gravel in one tub, and place the small plastic scoop inside. On the other side of the balancing scales, put dry gravel in another tub with the small scoop, and next to it place a colander inside another large tub. Children can be encouraged to scoop gravel into the colander and then pour some water through it. For this purpose, place a small pitcher of water next to the colander. The amount of water you provide should depend on how big your tubs are, and whether or not the whole project is contained in one large sensory table. Place the picture sign in a prominent place. |

| directions | Encourage the children to experiment with the materials. Younger children may not be interested in making sure they fill their containers exactly to the top and have exactly the same amount in each, but they'll have a good time pouring water in the gravel, scooping it, and putting it into the scales. Make |

sure you keep some extra dry gravel on hand, in case the dry gravel at the experiment table also gets watered down. Ask the kids about what they're discovering.

SCIENCE:
Rock Scratch

objective   Facilitate the understanding that some rocks are harder than others.

materials   Shale samples and/or
Chalk pieces and/or
Pumice (you can get this at a drug store in the foot care section)
Other rocks
Paperclips
Picture sign saying: "What happens when you scratch the rocks?"

preparation   Pull one prong out from each paperclip to use for scratching. Spread all materials out on an activity table, including the activity sign.

directions   During the introductory activities, take one rock and one paperclip. Scratch the rock and ask whether it made a mark or not. Tell children that some rocks are harder than others, and that if they would like to do their own scratching experiment, the things they need are on the activity table. Then watch the children explore, and talk to them about their findings.

MATH:
Rock Sorting

objective   Facilitate sorting practice, and for older children, a rational counting exercise in teens; develop sense of autonomy and self-esteem through one-person work station.

materials   A collection of pebbles
A collection of medium sized rocks
A collection of large rocks

Three containers proportionate to the rocks you have
A very large tub or tray
Picture sign saying: "Would you like to sort the rocks?"
"One person may be here" sign
Writing sheets (described below)

preparation   Mix all the rocks up and place them in the bin or
tray. This project can easily be arranged on the
floor. Place each sign indicating each size rock on
the appropriate container, and above them, on a
chair perhaps, or hung on the wall, place the sign that
says, "Would you like to sort the rocks?", as well as a sign
that says "One person may be here." Place pens and photocopies of
the writing sheets next to the tubs. To make the writing
sheets, write the sentences "How many
small/medium/large rocks do you count?" on a sheet of
paper, and above each sentence, draw a picture of the
corresponding container and label it small, medium or
large. Photocopy the sheet. Since small, medium and
large are subjective judgments, the answers on the writing
sheets will differ. This is perfectly fine. In determining what
constitutes small, medium and large, kids are deciding their own standards and
making their own judgments.

directions   During introductory activities, tell the children
the sorting story in the spool unit on page 24, but
substitute the word rock, stone or pebble for spool.
Let the kids know that if they would like to do their
own sorting, the materials are available on an activity table.

SOCIAL STUDIES:
Rock Climbers

objective   Facilitate the understanding that in many endeavors, people depend
on each other.

materials   Pictures or books about rock climbing (see below)
Pictures that show people connected by rope as they ascend
   slopes or rock faces (Difficult as it can be, try to get pictures
   that show women climbers, and climbers from diverse cultures)

preparation   Arrange the books and pictures in a place where the children can look over
them at their leisure. One book which has many pictures of climbers
connected by rope is *Mountain Climbing* by Jim Hargrove and S. A. Johnson,
Lerner Publication Co., 1983.

directions   A day or two after the books have been out, mention them during one morning's introductory activities. Why are the people tied together with rope? What would happen if the climbers weren't connected, and one person slipped? Talk to the kids about the danger of tying themselves up in rope during pretend play, or trying to climb in a rope. Explain that the rock climbers use special equipment, special ropes, and that they have special training.

DRAMATIC PLAY:
Rock Land

objective   Facilitate the acting out of real life situations; facilitate interaction with other children; develop vocabulary.

materials   Rocks
Plastic or rubber monsters, dinosaurs, or wild animals
Fisher Price people and blocks
Toy Dump trucks

preparation   Set out chosen materials on the floor.

directions   Watch the children play. Engage in dramatic play with them if appropriate.

EXTENDING THE CONCEPT

social studies   Take a rope for everyone to hold onto, and go for a rope walk together, with everyone holding on loosely to the rope. (Beforehand, once again, ask the children if it's ever safe to tie a rope around themselves. Ask: "What would happen if you tied a rope around yourselves and someone tripped and fell? Is it safe to use a rope to climb down something? Emphasize again that rock climbers use special equipment, special ropes, and have special training.) When you get back from your rope walk, talk about how it was different from going on a walk without a rope. (Everyone stays together, no one gets left behind, everyone sees things at the same time.)

nature/ gross motor   To supplement their rock collections, take the children on a rock hunt one day. Give them plastic bags to put their rocks in. Talk to them first about never touching glass or tin.

art   Have children paint or decorate the rocks they find, and if they like, make pet rocks or rock people.

**fine motor/
sensory** With leftover sand and rocks from the sand and rock collage activity, provide tubs of sand, small rocks buried inside, and sifters and strainers. Tell the children there are special things to be found in the sand.

LITERATURE

Steig, William, *Sylvester And The Magic Pebble*, Windmill Books/Simon & Schuster, 1969 (A long story, but a very well written one.)
*Cole, Joanna, *The Magic School Bus Inside The Earth*, Scholastic Inc.. 1987
Synmes, Dr. R. F., *Rocks And Minerals*, Alfred A. Knopf, 1988 (Excellent picture book — wonderful photographs)
Simon, Seymour, *Volcanoes*, Morrow Junior Books, 1988
Lohf, Sabine, *Things I Can Make With Stones*, Chronicle Books, 1990

Creepy crawlies feelers and wings, tickle and prickle on somebody's skin.

THEME: insects and spiders

My most valuable tool for teaching this unit is a collection of rubber, anatomically correct insects that accurately resemble insects and are very realistic looking. I've listed locations for buying these in the Resources Section. Alternatively, you can usually buy cheap packs of ants/flies/spiders in supermarkets, but beware of plastic spiders with fewer than eight legs. My students have literally played for hours with the rubber bugs, which have a lot more appeal than the cheap plastic ones, so I do recommend them as an investment. In regard to live insects, I don't like bringing them into the classroom because too often delicate legs and bodies get mangled and mashed, or the insects don't get the food they need for long term visits. I prefer to go on nature walks and spot insects in their natural habitats.

INTRODUCTORY ACTIVITIES

ATTENTION GRABBER

Put your plastic or rubber bugs in a paper bag, and invite the children to feel what's inside, and guess what it is. After some guessing time, empty out the contents of the bag.

INTRODUCTORY DISCUSSION

objective Introduce the theme; develop speaking and listening skills.

materials Insect rhyme
Photographs of insects
Drawings of insects

preparation You can find photographs of insects in *National Geographic* and other nature magazines.

directions Show children some photographs and drawings of bugs. What kinds of different bugs can they see in the pictures? Ask the children about insects that they've seen.

MOVEMENT: Bug Rhyme

objective Develop cognition by memorization of words and movements; have fun with words and actions.

materials Insect rhyme

directions Start by using your hands and fingers for the movements. For "Creepy crawlies," move your fingers like an insect. For "feelers," put an index finger on each side of your head. For "and wings," flap your arms like wings. For "tickle and prickle on somebody's skin," brush your fingertips on the back of your arm or hand. Say the rhyme with your eyes closed while brushing your finger tips on the your skin. Ask the kids whether it feels like a real bug. Instead of "somebody's skin," suggest that the children use their own names. For whole body movement, crawl on the ground and then for "feelers and wings," pretend to take off into the air. For "tickle and prickle on somebody's skin," pretend to land on an imaginary person.

MUSIC:
Eensy Weensy Spider

objective   Develop appreciation for music; help children feel good about their singing voices; facilitate experimentation in using voices in different ways.

materials   Small plastic spiders obtainable in supermarkets. (optional)

directions   Sing Eensy Weensy Spider using the plastic spiders. Sing it in a very squeaky voice, ordinary voice, and then very deep voice. Use the small, plastic spiders for the squeaky voice, two fingers on each hand for the medium voice, and your whole hands and all your fingers to make a giant spider when you use the deep voice.

ACTIVITY CENTERS

ART/LANGUAGE:
Bug Books

objective   Develop creative expression; develop all facets of language: reading, writing, speaking and listening skills.

materials   Fairly wide, long strips of light green paper, each about two feet long, and six inches in depth.
Markers
Crayons
Teacher's marker

preparation   Fold the strips of green paper accordion style, making sure each panel is roughly the same page size as all the others — about 6" long. Cut slashes all along the top to simulate grass, making some cuts at different angles. The cuts that you make should be about 2" in length. Make one for each child. Make a sample book yourself by drawing pictures of bugs in your book, or by gluing in photographs, and then write some words about them on each panel of the book.

directions   Take the children out on the grass with your rubber bugs and your sample bug book. Sitting down on the grass, and using it for the story's setting, tell the children the story on page 88 with your rubber bugs. As you tell this story, move your caterpillar in a large circle in the grass so that the caterpillar ends up in the same spot he started from. Use two of the same kind of rubber bug for the father and son. Many rubber bugs come in various sizes; I have a big caterpillar and a small one, which are perfect for this story. Again, if your collection has different insects than the ones mentioned here, change the story's words to fit the bugs you do have. Also, give each character a different voice. I've included suggestions based on how I usually tell the story, but you may have more fun with the story by telling it in your own creative way. Afterwards, ruffle the simulated grass of your bug book, and ask the kids what they think it is. They may guess that it's grass. Tell them you decided to make a bug book, and read them your story. When you go back indoors, show the kids the materials on the table and ask them what they could do with them. To develop writing skills, take the story dictation of young children. Older kids will probably want to write their own words. To develop speaking and listening skills, read their stories back to the children, and then ask them to be the ones to read/tell you their story from the beginning. Reverse the order of this as appropriate. You could also have each child read or tell her/his story for the other children during the next morning's introductory activities.

story   Once upon a time there was a little baby caterpillar who was born, and fell asleep. While he was asleep, his father went looking for a leaf for his baby to eat when he woke up. Well, the baby caterpillar woke up while his father was searching for food, and when the baby caterpillar didn't see his Dad anywhere, he decided to go look for him himself. Well, the baby caterpillar went along and went along, until he met someone. [Move caterpillar through grass, and move centipede in opposite direction, towards caterpillar.]

The baby caterpillar said, [baby voice] "Hmmmm. You're thin and long, just like me. Are you my father?" [Squeaky voice] "No," Centipede said, "I'm a centipede. I'm not your father." So the baby caterpillar went along, and went along until he met someone else. [Perform same actions as above, except use stag beetle.]

The baby caterpillar said, "Hmmm. You really don't look anything like me, but could you be my father anyway?" [Deep voice] "No," the stag beetle said, "I'm a stag beetle. I'm not your father." So the baby caterpillar went along, and went along and now he was beginning to get upset. "I want my father so much," he said to himself. "When am I going to find him?" But even though he was discouraged and sad, he kept trundling through the grass until soon he met a slug. [Perform same actions as above, except use the slug.]

"Hmmm," the baby caterpillar said, "you're long and you're thin, and you're also green, just like me. Are you my father?" [Slow, lazy voice] "No," said Slug, "I'm a slug. I'm not your father." So the baby caterpillar kept on looking through the grass, but now he was so tired that he had to stop and take a little rest. "I want my father so badly," he said. And just then, guess who came trundling through the grass?

[Move the larger caterpillar through the grass and have the kids guess.] And the father caterpillar said, "Oh, my baby caterpillar, I got you a lovely juicy leaf to eat." And the little baby caterpillar said, "Oh, Daddy, I was looking everywhere for you. I met Centipede and Stag Beetle and Slug, but none of them were you." And the father and son caterpillar had a juicy leaf for their juicy lunch and then they took a nap. [Move caterpillars as if they're eating the grass and then laying down to sleep.]
THE END.

ART:
Caterpillars

objective Develop fine motor skills; facilitate creative expression.

materials Egg cartons cut into single lines of three or four cups
Green glue — add green tempera paint to plain glue
Pipe cleaners cut fairly short — about 3" or 4"
Green, red and purple yarn cut into approximately 3/4" pieces

preparation Spread all materials out on the table. Make your own caterpillar ahead of time. You can use pipe cleaners for feelers if you like, and the yarn pieces can be glued on to make the caterpillar fuzzy.

directions You can do this art activity in conjunction with the book, 'The Very Hungry Caterpillar' if you like, and let each child hold your home-made caterpillar for as long as it takes you to read one page. Every time you turn a page, a child can pass it to the next. When you're finished with your chosen book, show the children the materials on the table and let them begin their creations.

DRAMATIC PLAY/SENSORY:
The Bug Party

objective Promote child to child conversation; help children connect actions with words; facilitate imaginative, verbal play.

materials Tubs or a large sensory table
Rubber bugs
Rocks
Stones
Water
Shells
Small styrofoam trays for boats

preparation   Set all materials in the sensory table or tubs.

directions   After telling the story below, encourage the children to explore the materials. They'll retell the original story, and make up their own. You may not have the same kinds of rubber bugs in your collection as I have in mine. If not, substitute the insects you do have when you tell the story. Use a loud hissing voice for the Scorpion character, and a soft hissing voice for the Spider, or whatever variation you like.

story   Once upon a time there was a mean, old scorpion who lived all by himself on a big rock. [Put scorpion on a rock.] The scorpion wouldn't make friends with any of the other insects. One day the spider decided to throw a party and she asked her friend, Slug, to go over and invite the scorpion because Spider was busy getting ready for the party. So Slug got on their boat [put Slug on styrofoam tray and float it over to the rock with the scorpion.] and went to visit Scorpion.

Well, Scorpion was hiding in the rocks, and before Slug could even get off the boat, Scorpion came rushing down from his rock as fast as he could and he said, [Use loud, hissing voice for Scorpion] "Go away and leave me alone. No one ever visits Scorpion on Scorpion Rock." Slug was so surprised and upset that he fell off the boat into the water [take the slug off the boat and drop it into the water] and had to swim all the way home because he was too frightened to climb back up on the boat. [Take the slug and move it back across the water as if it's swimming.])

When the boat came floating back [(bring tray back across the water], Spider asked Cockroach to go and try to get Scorpion to come to the party, because Spider was too busy gathering juicy leaves and flies to eat at the party banquet. Cockroach said, "Why are you bothering with that old Scorpion? He's always mean to everyone — just leave him alone." But Spider said, "I really want him to come and have some fun at my party. I don't want anyone left out. So whatever tricks he tries to pull, don't let Scorpion scare you." So Cockroach climbed onto the boat [put the cockroach on the tray and slowly bring it across the water to the scorpion's rock] and slowly, slowly Cockroach made her way over to Scorpion's rock.

But Scorpion was hiding in the rock and when Cockroach wasn't looking, Scorpion jumped out [move Scorpion so that it leaps out from behind the rock and onto the boat] and landed right on the boat and said, [in hissing voice] "Go away and leave me alone. No one ever visits Scorpion on Scorpion Rock.", and even though he'd decided he wouldn't be scared no matter what happened, Cockroach was so surprised and upset that he fell off the boat into the water and because he was too shaken to climb back up on the boat, he had to swim all the way home.

When the boat floated back, [bring boat back] Spider decided to go and invite Scorpion to the party himself. Cockroach and Slug said, "Oh, don't go — don't go — that terrible Scorpion will do something mean to you." But Spider wouldn't listen. So she got on the boat and floated over to Scorpion Rock herself. [Put Spider on the boat and bring the boat over.] Well, Scorpion was hiding in the rock, and when he saw Spider, Scorpion started to sneak up quietly, quietly behind her back. [Move the scorpion so that it comes up behind Spider] Scorpion was just about to hiss "What are you doing here on Scorpion Rock?", when Spider turned around and said, "Oh, hello! There you are." At first Scorpion didn't know what to do — he wasn't used to someone being so calm around him, — so he tried to scare Spider by saying: [hissing voice] "Go away and leave me alone. No one ever visits Scorpion on Scorpion Rock." And Spider said, "Nonsense. I'm here visiting you right now. I've come to invite you to the bug party." And Scorpion said, "Well, I won't go." Spider said, "Why not?" At first Scorpion wouldn't answer but finally he said, "None of the other bugs will like me. I have a hissing voice and long, crawly legs and they'll think I'm really mean. I decided a long time ago that if everyone was going to think I'm mean anyway, I might as well <u>be</u> mean." "Well," said Spider, "I have a hissing voice, and the bugs like me." "So you do." Scorpion said. "And," Spider said, "I have long, crawly legs, and the other bugs still like me." "So you do." Scorpion said. "Just come to the party for a little while," Spider said, "and if you don't have fun, you don't have to stay."

So they both went over to the party on the boat [put the scorpion and spider on the tray and float it over to the other rocks] and all the other bugs started arriving for the party and even though they were a little afraid of him, they were all nice to Scorpion because Spider had asked them to be and Scorpion had such a good time that he even sang a song and danced a dance for them [move scorpion as if it's dancing and sing like a rock singer — this never fails to make my kids giggle:]

'I'm really not mean, I'm just the Scorpion machine./Whoa whoa whoa/
A party is fun, and here I am at one./Whoa whoa whoa/
The bugs gave me a chance, and asked me up to dance./Whoa whoa whoa/
And all the bugs stayed up all night singing and dancing and eating grass pie and it was the best party they'd had in those parts for quite some time.

MATH:
Bug Match

objective   Develop understanding of one-to-one correspondence; develop cognition in recognizing and matching similar shapes; develop all facets of a language: reading, writing, listening and speaking.

materials   Rubber bugs
Light colored, legal-size construction paper
A black marker
Two styrofoam trays
A picture sign saying: "Would you like to match the bugs?"
Reduced photocopies of bug outlines
Two-person work table

preparation   My collection of rubber bugs includes: two slugs, one snail, three cockroaches, one stag beetle, two caterpillars, one scorpion, two spiders, and one centipede. It's ideal if you can acquire this diverse a collection or an even better one. Take half of your bugs, dividing them as evenly as possible (so you don't end up with all the spiders in one group, for example,) and spread the bugs out on the construction paper. Leave enough space for writing the name of each insect underneath its outline. Take a bold, black marker, and trace the outline of each rubber bug, and write its name underneath, in D'Nealian or printscript. Repeat this with the other half of the collection on the other piece of construction paper. Put the corresponding bugs in styrofoam trays, next to the piece of paper with the outlines they match. Put the sets of materials opposite each other, so that each child will be facing another while doing the project. Next to both, at the side, place the sign that says: "Would you like to match the bugs?" Make reduced photocopies of your bug outline sheets and add the question, "How many bugs do you count?" Draw a line underneath each outline for the children's answers. Place the sheets near the project, but on a separate tray with pens.

directions   Stand back and enjoy the children's exploration of the materials.

MATH:
How Many Legs?

objective   Facilitate rational counting; facilitate classification; develop all facets of language: reading and writing, speaking and listening skills.

materials   One large piece of butcher paper
One dark marker
A picture sign saying: "How many legs do the bugs have?"
Collection of rubber bugs

preparation   Look at your collection of bugs and draw a category for each insect, according to how many legs it has. Use three headings for each category: the written words, the numeral that represents the number of legs, and a drawing of a bug with that many legs. Put all the bugs on a tray, place them next to the butcher paper, and next to that, place the sign that says: "How many legs do the bugs have?" For older children, place pens and writing sheets with outlines of the bugs and their names (from last activity) next to the project.

directions   You may want to do this activity with the children as a group by saying something like, "Will anyone help me count the legs of these bugs? Gosh, I wonder where this one goes." This is especially suitable if some of your rubber bugs have more than ten legs. The speaking and listening skills develop as participants discuss and suggest where each bug belongs, as well as counting together how many legs on each insect — especially fun with the centipede. If the children are doing this project on their own, you may have to supervise to make sure that no single child grabs all the bugs to classify. Also, during the day's introductory activities, show the children the rubber bugs and differentiate between feelers and legs. My experience is that most kids are able to make this distinction, especially when it's emphasized that feelers are always at the top of the head, and are usually, (though not always — see the stag beetle) much smaller than legs. As the children write or color on the writing sheets, talk about the names of the bugs that are written there.

GROSS MOTOR/SOCIAL STUDIES:
Nature Walk/Insect Search

objective   Develop observation skills in searching for insect habitats; get some exercise in the fresh air; learn to respect the natural world; develop cognition by recalling a sequence of events.

materials   Yourselves and your eyes

preparation   I always talk to my kids before going on a bug search about leaving bugs where we find them, and not touching them, or taking them away from their habitats. Tell the children that "habitat" is the word for where things live. With younger children, together tap the word on your noses, on your knees, on your heads, with your feet or in any other interesting way that will help the children remember the word.

directions   As you walk along, encourage a discussion of all the insect habitats you may find. Where do spiders live? Where do ants live? Where do worms live? Also ask, what might we find flying in the air? During your walk, tell the children it's O.K. to gently turn over bark, rocks, or leaves to look for bugs, but that we will only use our eyes if we find anything, not our fingers. When you get back to home or school, discuss your nature walk to help the children recall the sequence of events.

SCIENCE/LANGUAGE:
Bug Display

objective   Allow close inspection of bugs; develop all facets of language: reading, writing, speaking and listening.

materials

Dead insects	Markers
Plastic magnifying glasses	Butcher or chart paper
Microscope (optional)	Plastic carry-out containers (optional)
Tagboard strips	

preparation   Well ahead of time, begin collecting any dead insects you find. Look under your bed, in dusty corners, in the garage, on window sills, and even keep your eyes peeled while you're walking outside. (Some people may feel squeamish about this, but the kids really do enjoy examining dead bugs.) When you have your collection, drop a row of beads of glue onto each tagboard strip, and drop an insect onto each bead of glue. Label each insect with marker, and if you don't know the name of the bug, don't worry — just explain this to the kids if they ask. Put the display on a table, and lay plastic magnifying glasses nearby. If you have a microscope that will examine more than slides, glue some of your bugs on small pieces of tagboard that will slide under the lens. Microscope use requires supervision and direction. In the course of being examined, the bugs will not stay intact very long. If you want to preserve them a little longer, you can cut down the sides of clear plastic carry-out containers and glue the remainder of the tray over the bugs so that the insects can be seen but not touched. Also, you may want to set some of your dead bugs aside, in case you have to replace the old, battered display with a new one. Another way to preserve your display is to cover each bug with Elmer's glue. When the glue dries it will be transparent, but the children may not get the best view of the bugs. Near the display, secure the butcher paper onto the wall at the children's eye level.

directions Encourage the children to examine the bugs. Make sure they know that all the bugs were dead when you found them, and that you didn't kill them. (You don't want to be remembered for all time as the Brutal Bug Slaughterer.) Encourage the kids to verbalize their observations, and make a language experience chart of their comments, using D'Nealian or printscript and alternating marker colors with each sentence. With older kids, encourage them to write their own comments. In the past, kids have asked me to write out their words on a separate piece of paper so that they could copy them onto the chart. You also may find this an appropriate approach. Read the comments back to the children.

EXTENDING THE CONCEPT

art Using the illustrations from some of the books you've used, (the ladybugs in *The Icky Bug Book* are perfect) draw simple outlines of bugs on paper, mix cornmeal with dry tempera, and provide glue. Let the children decorate their bugs by shaking the colored cornmeal onto glued areas. Provide plain paper and crayons, too, for kids who want to make their own outlines. Allow them to cut their bugs out if they wish.

sensory/ fine motor Extend the 'Creepy Crawlies' rhyme by tying string around one of your rubber insects and then tying the other end of the string to a stick. The rubber bug should hang down about a foot away from the stick. Let the kids take turns, one at a time, using it. The rest of the children sit in a circle with their eyes closed, and chant the rhyme. The person with the hanging bug stops behind someone and tries to tickle her/his hand with the rubber bug. Everyone says the rhyme until someone shouts: "I feel it!" and then it's that child's turn to do the tickling.

math Use your collection of plastic spiders to develop rational counting. Using chalk on black paper, draw a cobweb, and then put the picture flat down on a table. Put the spiders on it with a sign saying: 'Would you like to count the spiders?'

LITERATURE

Pallotta, Jerry, *The Icky Bug Alphabet Book,* Charlesbridge Publishers, 1986
Carle, Eric, *The Very Hungry Caterpillar,* Philomel, 1969
Pienkowski, Jan, *Oh My A Fly,* Price, Stern, Sloan, 1989 (Three dimensional)
Carle, Eric, *The Very Busy Spider,* Scholastic, 1984
Goor, Ron and Nancy, *Insect Metamorphosis,* Athenaeum, 1990
Hopf, Alice L., *Spiders,* Cobblehill Books, 1990 (Excellent photographs)
McGavin, George, *Discovering Bugs,* The Bookwright Press, 1989

Frothy, foamy,
water gushes
fast and full,
cascades and
rushes.

THEME: water

This is a very familiar theme to most parents and teachers, so I've tried to provide activities that stray a little from the common water projects that are normally suggested. Sensory tables are invaluable for this type of theme, but if you're working at home or in a school without one, tubs or fairly deep trays will also work. You can cut plastic, garbage bags open and spread them underneath the water tubs for greater protection.

INTRODUCTORY ACTIVITIES

ATTENTION GRABBER

Behind your back, keep a tub and a large pitcher of water. When all the children are gathered, ask them to cover their eyes with their hands, listen hard, and see if they can guess what it is that's making the sound. Slowly pour some of the water into the tub. They'll guess right away what the sound is and open their eyes. Ask them to cover their eyes again to see if they can guess whether you're pouring a lot of water or a little water. Try to pour a trickle. Then pour a lot. Listen to the children's comments.

INTRODUCTORY DISCUSSION

objective   Introduce the theme; stimulate thought; encourage descriptions of experiences with water and develop language skills.

materials   Water poem
Photographs of water from magazines — the ocean, waterfalls, rivers, ponds, rain. *National Geographic* magazine is a good source.

directions   Read the poem to the children at least twice. Looking at your water photographs, identify the words in the rhyme. What's froth? Foam? What does water look like when it gushes and cascades? Point out in your photographs other applications of these words. Ask the children if they've ever seen a waterfall. If you like, pretend with the children that you're standing under a waterfall. Talk about what you see, hear, and feel under your imaginary waterfall.

MOVEMENT/MUSIC/GROSS MOTOR:
Row Your Boat

objective   Facilitate gross motor exercise; help children enjoy singing; facilitate imaginative play.

materials   Yourselves
Ocean sounds on tape (optional)

To the tune of Row, Row, Row Your Boat, sing:
Row, row, row your boat, across the mighty ocean, waves go up and waves go down, they make a mighty motion.

preparation   Tell the children you're all going to take a pretend trip across the ocean, and point to your photograph of the sea.

directions   Ask everyone to find a partner, and sit facing each other, with your legs spread apart, feet to feet. Hold the hands of the person opposite you. Holding hands, lean forward and backward as you sing the song, and also try to lift your torso up for "waves go up," and to bring it down for "waves go down." Try it very slowly, and try it quickly. Explain to the children that motion means moving. Tell the children you think you see a storm coming, and that the ocean is going to get rougher. When the storm hits, try weaving from side to side at the same time that you lean backwards and forwards. Pretend to be seasick if you like. Stop holding hands for a while, and pretend to have oars, instead. Suggest that the children look down into the ocean from their boats. Ask them what they see. If you can get a tape of ocean sounds while you're doing this activity, it will greatly enhance it. Sometimes natural sounds tapes can be borrowed from the library.

ACTIVITY CENTERS

SENSORY/SCIENCE:
Water Shake

objective Provide sensory experience through working with water, liquid soap, and bubbles and shaking bottles; develop fine motor skills; facilitate scientific exploration of what happens when liquid soap and water are shaken up together.

materials Tubs or a sensory table
Small pitchers of warm water
A big pitcher of warm water for refills
Small pitchers of cold water
A big pitcher of cold water for refills
Liquid soap
Clear, plastic bottles with tops
Eye or medicine droppers and/or
Spoons and/or
Small funnels and/or
Very small, plastic bottles with caps
Puppet (optional)
Picture sign saying: "What happens when you put liquid soap in a bottle, add warm water, and shake?"

preparation Set out all materials. If you're using tubs, you may want to spread newspaper, plastic, garbage bags and/or a tablecloth on the table first. Make the sign in the appendix, and hang it up near the experiment. Before approaching the experiment, talk to the children about what will happen if you shake water in a bottle without screwing the cap on. I often use a puppet for these little talks — it's less boring. (Alexander the Alligator takes a bottle full of water and says "Wal, Ah jest think Ah'll give this here ol' bottle a little shake." Me: "No — Alexander — wait!" [To kids] "What'll happen if Alexander shakes this bottle with no top on it?" Alexander screws top half on. Me: "Oh no! The top isn't all the way on, Alexander." [To children] "What'll happen if he shakes it now?")

directions Help the children read/interpret the activity sign if they ask you what it says. As the children pour out the results of their water shake, ask: "Do you think it's frothy and foamy?" Provide cold water for rinsing their bottles out, and encourage them to see whether warm or cold water makes more bubbles.

SCIENCE:
Floating Raisins

objective Facilitate observation of raisins rising and sinking in a volume of water; facilitate exploration of what combination of ingredients brings this about; facilitate fun with pouring; develop fine motor skills; facilitate rational counting; develop all components of language: speaking, listening, reading and writing skills.

materials
Tubs and trays, or a
    sensory table
Small pitchers of water
Large pitchers of water
    for refills
Measuring spoons
Raisins
Bowls
Baking soda
Vinegar
Spoons
Writing sheets
    (described below)
Pencils or pens
Small, see-through containers like
    disposable plastic cups,
or: Empty, plastic peanut butter
    containers
One large, empty tub
Puppet (optional)
Picture sign saying: "What happens
    when you put water,
vinegar and raisins in a container, and
    then add baking soda?"

preparation Set out the materials so that each child has a see-through container, and if you're not doing the experiment in a sensory table, so that the containers are set in tubs or on trays. This is very important because containers often overflow. Make sure that the bowls of baking soda, raisins, vinegar, and water are easily accessible to each child. (With a group of eight, I usually put out at least three containers of each item.) Put the large, empty tub in the middle of the table. This is for kids to dump the contents of their containers in when they want to begin the experiment again. Often the raisins will continue to rise and sink in this debris tub, and this also makes for interesting observations. Your picture sign will have to show the containers you're using, and you'll want to make sure the water and vinegar are in very different, distinctive containers so that the symbols on the sign are as clear as possible. To make the writing sheets, draw a picture to illustrate each of the following questions: "How many raisins float up?", and "How many raisins sink?" One way to do this is to draw your container, first with the raisins floating and second with the raisins on the bottom. Place the writing sheets and pencils near the experiment, but not close enough that the paper will get wet. There is no set amount of vinegar and soda to be used in this experiment. Part of the process involves the children's discovery of which different mixtures and proportions produce which different results. Older children quickly discover that the more vinegar and soda they use, the more dramatic the reaction.

directions If the children ask you what the sign says, help them to read/interpret it. Encourage them to mix and explore the different materials. As the air bubbles that are created by the vinegar/baking soda reaction attach themselves to the raisins, and as the raisins begin to rise up and sink back down in the water, encourage the children's observations, (although I usually find that not much encouragement is needed!) Lots of language usually accompanies this experiment. After doing the experiment several times, older children are often interested in using the writing sheets to make a mark for every rising raisin, a mark for every sinking raisin, and then tallying the results. Younger children like to use them to scribble on, or to make invented letters. Near the end of the experiment, it's fun to take out your puppet and use it to ask the kids about the experiment and what they're doing.

LANGUAGE/MATH:
The Magic Water Well

objective Facilitate an understanding of comparative sizes; facilitate rational counting; expand vocabulary; stimulate children to use their language skills by retelling the original story and telling new ones.

materials   The flannel board story on page 102
Flannel board pieces on pages 229, 230
Small table
"Two People May Be Here" sign

preparation   Set out the materials on the table, and hang the sign in a visible place.

directions   Tell the children this story during your day's introductory activities. Then let them know that the flannel board, and flannel board pieces will be available for them to play with in the room, during free play time. I always hear some great new stories when my kids play with flannel board pieces. It may seem like there are a lot of pieces to this story, but except for the people, each piece is only a shape cut out of felt or other material. If you don't have time to color in the people, you can follow this easy method for making each character a little different: to give the parents and children differently colored clothes, put glue on the pieces, and sprinkle a different color of glitter on each one. To make the saplings and treehouse, just reduce the patterns for the tree and house on a photocopier. You can make the broken saw by copying the saw pattern and ripping it in half.

story   [Beforehand, put the house, the two saplings, and the broken saw on the board.] Once upon a time, a long time ago, there was a mother and father and their three children: Nishi, Karuna and Harsh. [On the flannel board, put each character as s/he is referred to.] There was just one thing that these children wanted in all the world, and that thing was a tree house. They had once read a story about a tree house, and they thought it must be the most wonderful thing to have; a place where you could be high up in the trees, all cozy and safe. Every day they asked their parents [move children to face parents] if they could have a tree house, and their parents always said exactly the same thing: "In the first place, we have no tree big enough to hold a tree house. In the second place, we have no tree big enough to give us the wood to build one, and in the third place, our saw is broken, so we have nothing to cut with." And that was always the end of that.

One day a tired, hungry, and very mysterious traveler [put traveler on flannel board] came by their house at dinner time. She said, "Please, I am so tired and hungry. Can you spare a scrap of food?" And so the children's parents gave her a good, hot meal. The very mysterious traveler asked for a drink, and they told her where the water well was. When the traveler returned from the well, she said: "I have rewarded you for the dinner you gave me. I have turned the water in your well into magic water. It will do magical things for you, but listen carefully: the water will only be magic for your first three visits to the well, and you must use this magic scoop to fill your containers." And the traveler handed them a tiny, magic water scoop, said goodbye, and headed down the road. [Put the scoop on the board.]

Everyone was very excited and they spent a long time talking about what they wanted to do first with the magic water. They thought they would like a swimming pool to swim in, in the long, hot summer days, and so because Nishi begged to be allowed to get the magic water and bring it to the house, her father gave her the tiny, magic scoop, a large container, and sent her to the well. [Put large container and scoop on the board, near the largest child. Put the water well on the board, some distance from the house, and move Nishi character towards it.] Nishi had to use that scoop once, twice, three times, four times, five times, six times before her large container was full of the magic water. [Move scoop as if it's scooping deep into the well, and have the kids count with you, or let the kids come up and take turns doing this as you tell the story.] Nishi was carrying that large container of magic water oh so carefully, [turn Nishi character to face the house, away from the well] but on the way home, an awful thing happened. She stumbled and dropped her container. [Move container as if it's falling.] All the magic water spilled out onto a nearby sapling, which is the word for a baby tree, and when her large container hit the ground, it broke. She went home crying, and everyone comforted her. They were sad too, because now they only had two visits left to get the magic water.

Karuna begged and begged to be allowed to get the magic water to make the swimming pool, and so finally everyone said she could, but they told her to be very, very careful, and not to trip on her way back home. Her mother gave her the tiny, magic scoop, and a medium sized container. [Put the scoop and medium sized container near the medium sized child.] When Karuna got to the well, it took her one scoop, two scoops, three scoops, four scoops to fill her medium sized container full of magic water. [Use scoop as above.] Karuna was carrying that medium sized container of magic water oh so carefully, but on the way back home, a terrible thing happened. The wind blew the door of the house so hard that it slammed shut, [move door flap as if it's slamming] and the loud bang scared Karuna so much, that she jumped, and dropped her medium sized container. [Move container as if it's falling.] It broke, and all the magic water spilled out onto another sapling, which, if you remember, is the word for a baby tree. Karuna, too, went home in tears.

Harsh said that since his sisters had been allowed to try to get the magic water, that he should be allowed to try, too. His parents said there was only once chance left, and that it was too important. They would go themselves. But Harsh begged and pleaded and promised he would bring back the magic water safe and sound if only they would let him try, so finally they agreed, but they asked him to be more careful than he had ever been in his life, and they told him all the things to watch out for. His father gave him the tiny, magic scoop, and a small container. [Put small container and scoop by smallest child and then move these pieces towards the well.] Harsh went to the well, and it took him one scoop, two scoops to fill his small container. [Use scoop as above.] Harsh was carrying his small container of magic water oh so carefully, but a dreadful thing happened to him on the way home. The old, broken saw was laying hidden in the grass, and Harsh tripped on its handle. [Move character accordingly, and move container as if it's falling.] His small container fell and broke, and all his magic water spilled onto the saw.

Now that all their chances to get the magic water were gone, everyone was very sad, and they all went to bed early because they felt so bad. But the next morning, when they came out of the house, guess what they saw? The magic water had worked on everything it had spilled on. The two saplings had grown into huge, strong trees, [replace saplings with trees] and the saw was mended and shining like new [replace old saw with new one]. At first everyone was too amazed to say anything. But then Karuna said, "Wait a minute! We have two big trees, and a brand new saw! We could build a tree house!" And so they got over their disappointment that all the magic water had been spilled, and together, the whole family chopped down one tree, [take down one large tree] and used the wood to build a tree house in the other [put tree house shape in the other tree]. The children played in that leafy tree house every day, all summer, [put children's shapes on treehouse shape] and they never forgot the mysterious traveler who had made their water magic.

THE END.

MATH/SENSORY:
Magic Water/Container Count

objective Facilitate rational counting; facilitate measuring and comparing; develop fine motor skills; provide sensory experience with colored, glitter water; develop all components of language: speaking, listening, reading and writing skills.

materials Flannel board story from above activity
One color of food coloring
Glitter
A sensory table or large tubs and trays
Several uniform large containers, uniform medium sized containers, uniform small containers, and even smaller ones for scooping. (Coffee scoops, perhaps.)

preparation Use the flannel board story in the language activity below during introductory activities on the day that you put this math activity out. The story, besides creating extra interest in the activity, also gives it more meaning. Put some food coloring and glitter in the water, and the containers in it also. On a nearby separate table, place writing sheets and pens.

directions After telling the children the flannel board story 'The Magic Water Well,' tell the children there might be some magic water right there in your home or classroom and ask them to look for it. When they find the colored glitter water, stand back and watch the kids work. Some kids may actually measure how many scoopfuls of a small container fill a larger container, and will write their answers on the writing sheets. Some may choose to explore and play by simply pouring and emptying, and that's a good learning activity too.

LANGUAGE/ART:
Water Books

objective   Facilitate creative expression; develop fine motor skills; develop all components of language: speaking, listening, reading and writing skills.

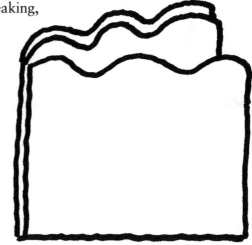

materials   Light blue construction paper
Dark blue construction paper
A stapler
Markers
Scissors
Magazines
Glue

preparation   To make the blank water books, cut a wavy line off the top of several sheets of light blue paper, and do the same with the dark blue. Your pieces of paper should be about one foot across, and six inches down. You'll want the peaks of the waves in the dark blue paper to appear in the troughs of the waves of the light blue paper. You can accomplish this when you start to cut your first wave out of dark blue paper, by making the first cut along the side an upward cut, and by making your first cut in the light blue paper a downward cut that starts at the top corner. Lay light blue on top of dark blue, fold and staple. Look through *National Geographic* and/or other magazines to find photographs of water. If you're working with young children, you can cut the pictures out yourself. If you're working with older kids, tear pages out and let the kids do their own cutting. Spread the blank water books and all other materials out on a table. To make your own water book, paste pictures of water into your blank book, and write words for your pictures. (Just to give you an idea, mine is as simple as this: "Water is pretty." [Magazine picture of the sun setting on the ocean.] "Sometimes I think I'd like to live on an island in the middle of a lot of water." [Picture of island.] "This man is standing in front of a dam. Dams keep water back. When people open a dam, the water rushes out." [Picture of semi-opened dam.] "People use water to wash their clothes and their bodies." [Picture of people doing these things.] "I use water for a lot of things. What do you use it for?")

directions For younger children, be available to take story dictation. Facilitate older children's use of invented spelling. Ask children if they'll tell you about their water books, and ask them if they'd like you to read them out loud. If you like, at the end of the day's activities, gather together again and have a "show and tell" of water books.

ART:
Water Drop Flowers

objective Facilitate creative expression; facilitate exploration of new, unusual materials; develop fine motor skills; facilitate exploration with mixing colors.

materials Eye or medicine droppers
Several colors of food coloring
Coffee filters
Small containers
A dish or pan
Optional: Plastic/rubber soap holders (the kind with many small suction cups)

preparation Arrange all materials such that every child has an eye or medicine dropper, and access to all other materials. In the small containers, add food coloring so that you have four differently colored batches of water. If you're using soap holders, provide a dish or pan of plain water for rinsing out the soap holders to begin a new design.

directions Make a sample flower yourself by using the eye or medicine dropper to put a drop of colored water directly onto a coffee filter. Show the children your water drop flower during introductory activities, and tell them how you made it. Children really enjoy watching the filters soak up the colors, but let them know they can use the materials in other ways too, if they like. (Some children just like to combine differently colored water to make new colors in the containers.) When the "flowers" are done, ask the children if they'd like to tape them up on the window so the light can show through. Optional: if you're using soap holders, invite the children to put drops in each suction cup. Some children will become engrossed in this activity alone, spending a long time making patterns and new colors. Others will take the next step, and press filters down on their soap holders after they've filled the tiny cups with the designs and colors they want. Encourage the kids to watch how the design and colors change when the filter is lifted off the soap holder.

ART:
Boats

objective   Develop fine motor skills; facilitate individual expression as well as creative planning and executing.

materials   Small to medium sized styrofoam trays
Triangular and rectangular sails cut out of sheets
Glue
Glue brushes
Popsicle sticks
Modeling clay
Small boxes
Spools
Paper shapes (See instructions on pages 17-18)
Markers
Flags, small rectangular ones and triangular ones
Skull and crossbones symbol at right on small circles of paper
Shallow pan of water

preparation   Make a boat yourself, first. Use the small boxes and spools for furniture which you can attach with glue. If you stick two blobs of putty onto your styrofoam tray about three inches apart, you can make a mast by sticking a popsicle stick into each putty blob and then by gluing a rectangular or triangular piece of sheet between the two posts. Also glue on a skull and crossbones symbol if you like, or any other form of decoration. Spread all activity materials on the work table.

directions   During introductory activities, show the children your boat. If you have some toy people, put them on your boat and tell a little story about them. (See sample story below) Let the kids know that if they want to make their own boats, the materials are available on a table. Fill a sensory table, or large tub with water, and add food coloring and glitter. Put one large rock at either end. Put your toy people on one rock. If you don't have store-bought people, make some out of spools. (See the spool unit, page 17) You'll also need the boat you made yourself, and three small shells for this story.

story Once upon a time, there were some people living on an island, and they were very unhappy living there. The dirt on the island was old and tired, and nothing would grow in it anymore. The people wanted to move to another island, but they couldn't, because they had no boat. One day though, the littlest person on the island shouted one morning: [Move smallest person as if she's shouting in excitement.] "Look! Look! A boat is floating towards us." [Put your self made boat in the water and push it towards the island.]

At first the people didn't believe the littlest person, but then one of them looked up, and sure enough, there was a boat floating towards them. They decided it must have been a pirate's ship once, because it had a pirate's flag on it. The people were very, very excited, because now they could look for another island to live on. They packed everything onto the ship, including three magic shells they had. These shells could only be used in times of trouble. The littlest person begged and begged to be allowed to hold one of these magic shells to keep it safe and sound, but the people said she was too little and that they didn't trust her. This made the littlest person cry very hard.

Finally they were ready to set sail, so they did, and they sailed and sailed for a long, long time, [move boat with people on it] and pretty soon they noticed that they had sailed into some magic water. It was magic, because if you even dipped your little finger in the water, you would fall fast asleep for many days.  Well, there was one person on the boat who had charge of one of the magic shells. [Hold one person and one shell so that it looks like the character is holding the object.] She was looking into the magic water, and couldn't resist touching it just the slightest little bit to see if it really worked. She couldn't believe it would really put her to sleep if she just touched the water with the very tip of her pinky finger. So she touched the water just for a split second with the very tip of her pinky finger and guess what happened? Instantly she fell asleep, and the magic shell slipped out of her hands and fell into the water. Now it was lost forever, and everyone was very upset. The littlest person said, "I wouldn't have lost that magic shell." But everyone only laughed at her.

The people sailed and sailed for many days more, [move boat in the water] and one afternoon the waves started to get very rough. The people held onto the boat as best they could, but all of a sudden the reason for the rough waves became clear. [Use one of your hands and arms to be a sea serpent. Use your hand for the head and your arm for the body. Wave your hand and arm to simulate the undulating coils of a serpent.] A terrible sea serpent appeared, and began making a dreadful sound. [Make a dreadful sound and snap your four fingers against your thumb to simulate the serpent's mouth.] The sea serpent was trying to eat the people and the boat. One person, who had charge of the other two magic shells, dropped them in his panic, and one of the shells fell off the boat, into the water, to be lost forever. But the littlest person kept her head, and grabbed the last magic shell. [Hold the smallest toy person and the last shell as if the character is holding the object.]

Quickly, she said: "Sneaky snaky serpent's call, shrink this worm to nothing at all!" There was a huge explosion of smoke, and when it had cleared, the terrible sea serpent had shrunk to only a very little water worm. [Wiggle your little finger in the water] The people said, "Oh, littlest person, we're so sorry we were mean to you and never let you help us. Will you forgive us?" The littlest person said she would forgive them, and the next day they found a new island to live on [move people and boat to the other rock] and lived happily ever after.
THE END.

DRAMATIC PLAY:
Boats and People

objective   Develop language; facilitate acting out of real life situations; facilitate child-to-child conversation; develop vocabulary.

materials   The self-made boats, after they've dried
Fisher-Price people, spool people,
or small, plastic or rubber animals.
A sensory table or tubs of water
Blue food coloring — optional

preparation   Add blue food coloring to the water if you like. Put the children's self-made boats on a table near the water. Put the people or animals on the table, too. Sometimes it's fun to put rocks or shells in the water to make it more interesting. Put out some empty styrofoam trays too, for kids who might not have made a boat.

directions   Stand back and watch!

SOCIAL STUDIES:
Picture Hanging

objective Facilitate an understanding that all people around the world depend on water; develop self-esteem and a sense of autonomy by encouraging children to choose their own place to hang a picture; develop speaking and listening skills.

materials Pictures of people around the world using or traveling in water. *National Geographic* is an excellent source for obtaining these; some of them may be left over from your first day's introductory activities.

preparation Put the pictures on a table, making sure there's at least one for each child to hang up. Put pieces of masking tape along the edge of the table. During the day's introductory activities, tell the children they can pick one picture, and that they can hang it anywhere on the wall that they would like to.

directions After the kids have hung the pictures, and after the day's activities, walk around together and talk about the pictures. Talk about what the people are doing, and how they are using or traveling in the water. Ask the kids if they think anyone can live without water.

EXTENDING THE CONCEPT

art Before the children make their boats, cut out sail shapes from an old sheet. Add enough food coloring to several containers of water to make batches that are strong and dark in color. The children can dip the sheet sail shapes into the colored water and then let them dry. When they make their boats, they'll have colored sails to use.

sensory/ movement If you can borrow or buy a tape of a rainforest shower, play it on a tape player and pretend with the children that you're seeking shelter from the rain, in the forest. Maybe you stand under a tree, and water drips down your neck. Maybe you find a cave, and stand in the opening watching the shower. Maybe you crawl under a bush and wait for the shower to stop. You may not need any of these ideas — the kids may lead the experience.

math/science When doing the water shake, a fun variation is to punch holes of varying diameters and at various levels on the plastic bottles. Compare the streams of water that flow out of them.

LITERATURE

Kovacs Buxbaum, Susan, *Splash! All About Baths*, Little Brown & Co., 1987

Kalman, Bobbie, & Schaub, Janine, *Wonderful Water*, Crabtree Publishing, 1992 (Excellent photographs. With younger children, talk them through the book.)

Schmid, Eleonore, *The Water's Journey*, North-South Books, 1989

*Murphy, Bryan, *Experiment With Water*, Lerner Publications Company, 1991

Westberg Peters, Lisa, *The Sun, The Wind And The Rain*, Henry Holt & Co., 1988

Teaching From
FOOD

Oranges

Peanuts

Lemons

Noodles

Eggs

Juicy oranges
dribble and squirtle,
spume and spray and
dripple and spurtle.

THEME: oranges

Because oranges are so juicy, and have such a distinctive smell, they lend themselves perfectly to sensory-motor activities. Also, they're easy to pick up at the supermarket along with your regular shopping. The first science/sensory, language, math and art activities are a sequence of projects which stem from, and relate to, each other. Some require teacher involvement, but this won't detract from the child-initiated nature of the curriculum, since the kids still have the power to choose whether or not to participate.

INTRODUCTORY ACTIVITIES

ATTENTION GRABBER

Hide an orange behind your back, and when all the children are gathered, tell them you have something that rolls, but is not a ball. Give them more clues to help them guess what it is. Tell them it's juicy and that you can eat it. Your last clue might be that it's orange. When the kids guess the answer, let them pass the orange around.

INTRODUCTORY DISCUSSION

objective Introduce the theme; stimulate language development; develop listening and speaking skills; develop vocabulary through use of rhyme.

materials Orange rhyme

directions Read the rhyme to the children at least twice. Ask them if they like to eat oranges. What drink is made from oranges? Go over each verb in the rhyme, and ask the kids what they think the word means. Talk about the real word each made-up word comes from: squirt for squirtle, spurt for spurtle, drip for dripple. Is dribble a real word? What does it mean?

LANGUAGE:
Word Sounds

objective Facilitate self-awareness and fun with pronunciation.

materials Orange rhyme

directions Tell the children you're going to try to say the words in the rhyme as hard as you can, using your whole mouths. Suggest that they put their finger tips very lightly on their lips while they do it, to feel what their lips do when they say the words. Say: "Dribble. Squirtle. Spume. Spray. Dripple. Spurtle." Encourage the children's comments after the exercise.

MUSIC/MOVEMENT:
Musical Orange

objective Develop listening skills; develop motor skills; develop hand/eye coordination; have fun!

materials An orange
A tape recorder or record player
Music on a tape or record

directions Roll the orange back and forth to each other, making sure that everyone gets a turn. Tell the children that when the music stops, whoever has the orange has to hold it under her/his chin with no hands — be prepared for lots of giggling when you get to this part.

ACTIVITY CENTERS

SCIENCE/SENSORY:
Peeling And Eating Oranges.

objective   Facilitate sensory exploration of an orange; develop fine motor skills; encourage scientific exploration; use and discuss sense of taste.

materials   Enough oranges so that each child can have one
A tub of soapy water
Paper towels
A knife

preparation   Cut incisions in each orange to make it easier for the kids to peel them. Put the oranges in easy reach of the children, but ask them to wash and dry their hands, using the tub of soapy water and paper towels, before they touch and eat them.

directions   Suggest to the kids that as you peel and eat the oranges, you all keep your eyes and ears open for some of the things in the rhyme. Ask the kids: "Does anyone feel or see a squirt or a spurt? Do you think that's the same as a squirtle or spurtle? Do you feel a spray of juice from your orange when you peel it? What does the peel feel like? What does the orange feel like? How does it taste? Is it juicy?" Also, ask the children to notice what they smell.

LANGUAGE:
Sensory Chart

objective   Show the children that their words are important; stimulate verbalization of experiences; develop reading skills.

materials   A large piece of butcher or chart paper
Two differently colored markers

preparation   Put the blank chart up on the wall near the table where the children will be peeling and eating the oranges. When you write down their words or sentences, alternate marker colors to make it easier for the children to identify individual sentences, and use printscript or D'Nealian, so kids can identify separate words. Use quotation marks, and write the children's names after their words.

directions   As the children are peeling their oranges, and as you ask them the questions suggested in the science/sensory project above, write down the children's comments. When everyone who wanted to has contributed, read the chart back to the children. Move it down to the kids' eye level and leave it up for a day or two.

MATH:
Orange Peel And Seed Count

objective   Facilitate rational counting; develop reading and writing skills.

materials   Small plastic zip lock bags
Pens
Writing sheets with two columns: "How many peels?" and
"How many seeds?"
Marker
Sticky labels

preparation   Have these materials available near the table at which the kids are peeling and eating their oranges.

directions   Suggest to the children that they keep their seeds and peels. Tell them they can put them in the plastic bags, and using the sticky labels, either write their names on for them, or have them do it themselves. Ask the kids if they'd like to count their seeds and peels. Show them the writing sheets. If they want to, they can use them to write down the number of seeds and peels they have, and can then include their writing sheets in their bags.

ART:
Orange Peel And Seed Collage

objective   Develop fine motor skills; facilitate creative expression.

materials   Seeds and peels from above activity
Paper plates   Construction paper
Glue   Glitter
Glue brushes   Sequins
Scissors   Spangles
Markers

preparation   On the paper plates, write in D'Nealian or printscript: "Guess what I ate today!" Glue your own orange peels and seeds onto one plate. When the children are beginning to finish eating their oranges, show them your plate, and say, "I have a riddle for you. My plate says: 'Guess what I ate today!'" When the children guess that the answer is an orange, ask them what's on the plate that helped them guess.

directions   Allow the children to freely use the materials on the table. You may want to provide some plates with the above question written on them, and some that are blank. The construction paper, markers, glitter, sequins and/or spangles allow the kids to take the project in a different direction if they like.

MATH/DRAMATIC PLAY:
Orange Stand

objective   Facilitate weighing, counting and comparing exercise; develop vocabulary and self-expression; connect dramatic play words with actions; provide the opportunity to interact with other children.

materials
Oranges
Balancing scales
Bags
Play cash registers
Pennies and/or nickels
Pens
Markers
Notebooks that simulate receipt books
Baskets
"Special" signs (supermarkets will often donate blank special signs.)
Photographs of oranges cut out from supermarket ad inserts
Children's aprons

preparation   Create an orange stand by setting out the materials. On blank signs, write out some specials and put them up on the wall with the photographs of oranges from the ad inserts. Lay out the blank signs and markers for the kids to write on. Save these oranges to use for the orange roll activity and juice squeezing activity below. If you like, during introductory activities, read *What's It Like To Be A Grocer*, by Shelley Wilks, published by Troll Associates.

directions   Stand back and let the kids explore the orange stand. When appropriate, grab a basket and some pennies, and be a customer. I like to say something like: "Hello! I need two pounds of oranges today because I'm going to make a big fruit salad."

GROSS MOTOR:
Orange Roll

objective   Develop gross motor skills; have fun!

materials   Large cardboard tubes or plastic tunnels
Medium sized boxes
Oranges

preparation   Cut out most of the bottom of each box. The oranges are going to roll straight through the box tunnels, but the entire bottom can't be cut out, or the box may collapse, so leave a margin of cardboard around the top and two sides. Set the cardboard tubes and box tunnels around the room, and set a bowl of oranges in the middle. You may want to line several tunnels up end to end to make a larger tunnel.

directions   Invite the kids to roll the oranges through the tunnels to each other. When you're finished with this activity, save the oranges for the Orange Squeeze activity below.

SCIENCE:
Orange Squeeze

objective   Develop hand and arm muscles; develop self-esteem and sense of autonomy through one-person work station; develop self-esteem through sense of accomplishment at making orange juice.

materials   Oranges (Use the oranges from the orange stand and orange roll activities above.)
An electric juice squeezer or a plastic, manual squeezer
A pitcher
A tub of soapy water
Paper towels
Picture sign saying: "Would you like to squeeze an orange and pour the juice into the pitcher?"

preparation   Cut all the oranges in half, put them in a bowl and set the bowl aside. Set the rest of the materials on a small table, with a sign that says: "One person may be here." Ahead of time, calculate how many orange halves each child may squeeze, and put that amount on the table. Before the children approach the table, remind them to cover their mouths if they sneeze or cough. Have the kids wash their hands in the soapy water before squeezing oranges. Save five or six oranges from this activity for the art project below — some that have been squeezed, and some that haven't.

directions   Electric squeezers are much easier for kids to use, but even with one of these, younger children may need you to hold the squeezer while they press the orange down on it. As you help, talk to the children about how the orange squeezer is working. How does it make the juice come out? When kids are finished squeezing, show them the pitcher, and encourage them to pour their juice into it. Save this juice for the next day's Social Studies activity below.

SOCIAL STUDIES:
Making Juice Together

objective   Reinforce the concept of the advantage of cooperating and doing things for each other.

materials   The juice from the above activity
The juice from one orange in a clear, plastic cup
Small pitchers
Cups
Black marker
Garbage can or plastic tub
Picture sign saying: "Orange juice we squeezed. Would you like to drink some?"

preparation   Set the pitchers and cups on a table. Draw a black line on the outside of each cup which indicates how much juice each person can pour (so that there's enough for everyone. You may have to squeeze extra oranges to ensure that you do have enough.) Put a garbage can or plastic tub near the table for the empty cups.

directions   During the introductory activities of the day, show the children the juice of one orange. Say: "This is the juice from one orange that I squeezed. Do you think this is enough juice for everyone to have some?" Next, show the children the pitcher of juice they squeezed the previous day. Ask, "How did we get so much juice?" Compare the amount of juice in the pitcher with the amount of juice in the cup. Talk about all the children who squeezed oranges, and how much juice it made. Ask the children, "Is this enough for us all to have some?" Tell them how glad you are that everyone helped to make juice for each other.   Tell the children that each person may pour <u>one</u> cup of juice for her or himself. Show the kids the black line on each cup and discuss why it's there. Ask: "Is it O.K. to put this much juice in your cup? (Point to a spot higher than the line.) Why not?" Talk about where the cups should go when they're empty. Also, talk again about the importance of covering your mouth when you sneeze or cough, especially around food. Show the kids where the table with the pitchers and cups is, and during free play, encourage them to pour themselves some juice and drink it. Is it good? Supervise this activity fairly closely.

ART:
Orange Prints

objective Facilitate experimentation with unusual art materials; facilitate sensory experience; develop creative expression.

materials Squeezed and unsqueezed orange halves from the juice squeezing activity above
Several colors of paint in shallow pans
Paint
Newspaper

preparation Set all materials out on a table.

directions Encourage the children to dip the orange halves in paint, and make prints with them.

EXTENDING THE CONCEPT

science Take orange peels and put them in the sun. What happens to them? Compare them to fresh peels.

language/ listening skills Read the orange rhyme, and ask the kids to listen for 'ssss' sounds. Ask them to stamp their foot every time they hear one, and read the rhyme again slowly. Ask the children to think of other words that have an 's' sound. Ask them to look around the room and find things with names that have an 's' sound. Ask them to listen to the sound their palms make when they rub them together. Can they hear a sound if they rub their finger tips together?

gross motor/ coordination During introductory activities, ask the children to pass the orange around the circle without using their hands.

LITERATURE

Jeunesse, Gallimard, *Fruit*, Scholastic, 1989
*Rogow, Zack, *Oranges*, Orchard Books, 1988
McGuire, Richard, *The Orange Book*, Children's Universe, 1992

Nutty peanuts,
gnash 'em,
crunch 'em,
crack those shells
and chomp 'em,
munch 'em.

THEME: peanuts

Even if unshelled peanuts are not so familiar to children, peanut butter usually is. This theme helps reinforce the connection between the two. Many supermarkets stock salted, unsalted, and roasted unshelled peanuts, as well as the more common shelled, bagged kind. One note of caution: C.P.R. instructors warn against giving children straight peanut butter on spoons — it's a leading cause of choking among kids. However, I've used peanut butter for activities in which kids spread it on celery or apple slices, and never had a problem. Also, to avoid choking during the peanut taste test, it's recommended that all peanuts be crushed first. Pounding peanuts is a fun activity for kids. Make sure you save all your peanut shells for art activities!

INTRODUCTORY ACTIVITIES

ATTENTION GRABBER

Put about a cup of unshelled peanuts in a brown paper bag and as the children gather, have them put their hands in the bag without looking, and guess what they're feeling. When everyone's had a chance to feel what's in the bag and guess its contents, pour the peanuts out. Let everyone take a peanut, shell it

125

and eat it. Tell the kids that peanuts with the shells on are called "unshelled" peanuts. After you shell one, tell the kids it is a "shelled" peanut because you've taken the shell off. The two words are so similar, that it will be confusing for young kids. Don't worry about this — the kids will be exposed to these two adjectives more and more as you work through the theme.

INTRODUCTORY DISCUSSION

objective   Introduce the theme; encourage comments, observations, and descriptions of experiences; develop speaking and listening skills.

materials   Peanut rhyme

directions   Before reading the rhyme, ask children if they like peanuts and peanut butter. Read the rhyme to the kids at least twice. Pretend to take peanuts out of a bag, shell them, pop them into your mouth, and gnash 'em. Talk to the children about what gnashing is. Pretend to crunch the peanuts, then chomp them, then munch them. Is there a difference?

SOCIAL STUDIES:
George Washington Carver

objective   Familiarize children with the work of George Washington Carver; help children understand that important, valuable discoveries and inventions are contributed by all groups in our society.

materials   Picture of George Washington Carver
Biography below
Butcher paper
Markers

preparation   Beforehand, post a picture of Carver and the butcher paper on a wall near the place where you'll be gathering with the children. Have the biography on hand.

directions   As you read the biography, stop to draw illustrations on the butcher paper. Afterwards, discuss Carver's obstacles and accomplishments with the children.

biography   Some brown skinned people are called 'black'. Some black people are African Americans, whose families came from Africa a long time ago. Pink skinned people are called "white." Once in America, white people went to Africa and kidnapped African people. They crammed them into ships, and brought them here. The African people were sold as slaves. The white owners treated the slaves like work animals. What do you think about that? It was during this time that a boy named George was born to a slave named Mary, on Moses

Carver's farm. As George grew up, people noticed that he was a very fast learner. He'd watch people knit, crochet, make medicine, tan hides, cure bacon and sew shoes, and then he'd say, "I can do that!" And when he tried, he usually could. George wanted to go to the local school, but he couldn't, because only people with pink skin were allowed to study there. So George went to a school for black children, eight miles away. When George had learned everything he could there, he left to go to another school. By this time, a war had been fought which was supposed to make all African Americans free. On his way to the new school though, George was stopped and beaten by some white men, because his skin was brown. Another time, he saw an African American man burned to death by some other white men. What do you think he felt then? When George grew up, he wanted to go to college, so he went to a university in Kansas. But when he tried to start classes, the principal wouldn't let him, because his skin was brown. How do you think he felt? George found another college that would let him be a student, and while he was there, he learned a lot. He spent a lot of his time learning all about plants — how they grow, how they get food, how they make more plants, and the best way to take care of them. Then, a friend of George's, Dr. Booker T. Washington, asked him to teach students all about plants at a new college he was starting in Tuskegee, Alabama. The young African American students who went there still couldn't go to school with whites. Some African American leaders thought that black people should use all their energy fighting for the right to go to school wherever they wanted. But George thought he could help his people by teaching at the new school, so he decided to go. On the train journey to the new school, he saw African Americans bending down over and over again to pick puffy white cotton balls to fill big sacks. They had to do this for hours every day. Do you think this would be fun? George saw them and thought, "This is why I'm going to teach at Dr. Washington's school. My people deserve a chance for something better, and I'm going to help them." And he did. George Washington Carver helped people learn how to feed their cows so they would give more milk, how to grow their own vegetables, how to raise chickens, how to make their own clothes and how to cook new kinds of dishes. Soon, the new school was a big success, and rich white people gave the school money, but these white people still wanted African Americans to live completely apart from them. Some African American leaders were angry about this, and felt that Dr. Washington and George were not helping their people in the right way. George chose to stay at the school and contine to teach. Then, something bad happened to farmers in the South. A small bug called a boll weevil was eating up the cotton. George told farmers to burn the cotton plants with bugs in them, and to plant peanuts instead. "Who will buy our peanuts?" the farmers asked. "What will people use all those peanuts for?" George set out to find an answer. In his laboratory, he cooked peanuts by boiling them, and then he mashed them, strained them, and dried them. He pressed oil from peanuts and found he could make peanut oil, as well as peanut butter, peanut flour, peanut milk, and five kinds of peanut soup. From peanuts George also learned how to make shampoos for hair and dyes for clothing. After all his science experiments, he showed that nearly three hundred useful things could be made from peanuts. When George Washington Carver died, he left behind him a museum in Tuskegee. In this museum, you can see beautiful flower paintings that he painted, as well as things that George invented from peanuts, cotton and sweet potatoes. Maybe you'll get to visit it one day. Some people feel that George Carver was a scientist who didn't fight for African Americans to be equal. Others feel that he was a scientist who chose his own way of helping people.

MUSIC/MOVEMENT:
There Was A Peanut

objective   Develop cognitive skills by memorizing words and connected actions; help children feel good about singing.

materials   To the tune of Yankee Doodle:
There was a peanut on the track,
it shook and then it shuddered,
'cause down the track there chugged a train
and made it peanut butter!

directions   For "There was a peanut on the track," use your index finger and thumb to pretend to put a peanut down on a track. For "it shook and then it shuddered," wrap your arms around yourself and shake and shiver. For " 'cause down the track there chugged a train," move both arms like train wheels at your sides. For "and made it peanut butter," slap/skid the palm of one hand against the palm of the other. After singing the song and doing the motions with

the children a few times, ask them what happened to the peanut on the track. How was it made into peanut butter?

ACTIVITY CENTERS

LANGUAGE/DRAMATIC PLAY:
Peanut Flannel Board Story

objective Facilitate creative use of language and invention of dramatic play situations; facilitate interaction between children; develop listening skills.

materials The flannel board pieces on page 231
Peanut song above
A flannel board
A "Two People May Be Here" sign

preparation You can use the flannel board pieces with the song during introductory activities. Another use is to have the kids themselves take turns at putting the flannel pieces up on the board while the rest of you sing. When you're finished, let the kids know that the flannel board will be available as an activity during free play. Make a sign that says: "Two (2) People May Be Here" and place it at the flannel board. For older kids, make a picture chart of the rhyme and hang it on the wall. Have paper, pens and markers available near the chart.

directions Stand back and enjoy listening to retellings of the original rhyme as well as new stories.

LANGUAGE:
Peanut Badge

objective Develop conversational skills; develop cognition by recalling past events.

materials Peanut badges

preparation An easy way to make these badges is to make photocopies of the sample at right, cut them out, and put masking tape loops on the back. If you want them to approximate the color of real peanuts, and you have time, you can trace them individually onto light brown construction paper. Write "Ask me what I did with peanuts today!" on some, and leave others blank for kids who want their own words on their badges. Put a peanut badge on yourself after you've done the taste test activity described below.

directions   When the children notice your badge, tell them what it says, and ask them if they would like one. Let each kid put his/her badge on by his/herself.

LANGUAGE:
Peanut Chart

objective   Develop self-esteem by having children's comments recorded; help kids understand that their ideas are important; develop speaking skills and vocabulary.

materials   A large piece of butcher or chart paper
Two markers of different colors

preparation   Put the paper up on the wall near the Peanut Taste Test activity below.

directions   As the children participate in the taste test below, ask for their comments. After the taste test, read the chart back to the kids.

SCIENCE/SENSORY:
Peanut Taste Test

objective   Develop awareness of sense of taste; develop awareness of varying textures; develop language use.

materials   Roasted, unsalted peanuts, a few unshelled
Roasted, salted peanuts, a few unshelled
Raw peanuts, a few unshelled
Popsicle sticks or plastic knives
Peanut butter
Small paper cups
Plastic spoons
Sturdy zip lock freezer bags
Children's mallets or anything they can use to pound
Older children: Coffee can and lid
Photocopies of ballots (described below)
Pens

preparation   Ahead of time, put the shelled peanut varieties in zip lock bags, and let the children pound them with the mallets to make sure all nuts are crushed into small pieces. Set out the variety of shelled peanuts in separate containers next to their unshelled counterparts and use signs to mark them. Nearby, place the paper cups and spoons. Put tiny dabs of peanut butter on popsicle sticks or plastic knives. (If the dabs are small, there shouldn't be any concern about choking.) The purpose of the peanut butter is to provide a comparison in texture as well as taste. Place chairs opposite the table of peanuts.

directions   Help the children spoon the crushed peanuts into the cups and as you do so, comment on whether the chosen peanuts are roasted, unroasted, salted or unsalted. To rule out any chance of choking, it's very important that after choosing their peanuts, the kids sit down to eat them. As you write down their comments on the language chart above, ask the kids questions like: Which is your favorite kind of peanut? Which one is the crunchiest? Do you like the roasted ones better than the raw ones? Do you like the salted peanuts better than the unsalted? Does the peanut butter feel the same in your mouth as the peanuts? You may not need to use any of these questions — sometimes comments and observations flow so fast that it's all you can do to write them down quickly enough. Other times, though, specific questions are handy for initiating the expression of ideas. For older children, make a ballot and photocopy it so that the kids can vote for their favorite peanut variety. One way to do this is to draw a peanut above a fire symbol with a plus sign and a salt shaker for roasted, salted ones, the same minus a salt shaker for roasted, unsalted, a plain peanut for raw, and a jar of peanut butter to symbolize peanut butter. You can find examples of these symbols in the Clip Art section. Under each picture, write the phrase that describes that variety of peanut. Under each kind, write "I like them" (followed by a smiley face) and "I don't like them" (followed by a frowny face) and make a line by each sentence for students to check. Lastly, have a line on the ballot sheet that says, "My favorite peanut is _____." Cut a slit in a box or in a plastic coffee can lid for a ballot box, and place the ballots near it with pens. During one day's introductory activities, take out the ballots and count them with the children.

SCIENCE:
Peanut Butter And Oil

objective   Facilitate the understanding that oil separates from substances; facilitate scientific observation; develop fine motor skills through measuring and stirring; elicit predictions and develop language skills.

materials Clear plastic containers — empty peanut butter containers are perfect
Peanut butter
Vegetable oil
Metal forks
Large spoons (tablespoon or bigger)
A medium sized bowl
Small bowls
Masking tape
A marker
Index cards
Pens
Picture sign saying: "What happens when you mix oil and peanut butter and let it sit for a few days?"

preparation Put all materials out on a table, with the sign. Put the peanut butter in the small bowls, so that several children at a time have access to it. Put a strip of masking tape on each container, so that you'll be ready to write each child's name on his/her cup.

directions During introductory activities, put peanut butter and oil in a container and stir together. Tell the children that you have a feeling that after a long time, something will happen to the peanut butter and oil and that you want to conduct a science experiment to see if you're right. Let the kids know that if they want to do their own science experiment with these materials, that the things they need are available on a table. When they approach, encourage the kids to put peanut butter in their containers with <u>many</u> large spoonfuls of vegetable oil, and to stir them together. Ask them if they can still see the oil. Suggest that you let the containers sit for a few days, and see if there's a change. (Certain brands of peanut butter may take longer than others.) Ask the children for predictions, and invite them to write their words on index cards, and leave them next to their containers. Take dictation from younger kids, and encourage older children to write or copy their own words. To help them express predictions, you could ask questions like: "What do you think will happen to the oil that you stirred in, if we let the peanut butter sit for a few days?" Take the containers out after five or six days. What did the oil do? Why?

MATH:
How Many Scoops?

objective   Facilitate rational counting; develop self-esteem and autonomy through one-person work station; develop reading and writing skills.

materials

Large plastic container of peanut butter
  A sensory table or tub
   Coffee scoop
   A plastic yogurt cup, or slightly larger
   container
  Tub of soapy water
   Paper towels
   Wastepaper basket
Small, one-person table
Pens
"One Person May Be Here" Sign
Picture sign saying: "How many scoops of
      peanut butter does it take to fill the
      container?"
   Writing sheets with same wording as
picture sign, but with a line added for answers.

preparation   In the sensory table or tub, place the peanut butter, coffee scoop, and empty container. If you're working with children who can count in teens, you may want to provide a larger container which will hold more scoops of peanut butter. This is a very messy activity, but kids <u>love</u> it. Nearby, place the writing sheets and pen, and also, on a chair or separate table, the soapy water, paper towels, and underneath, the wastepaper basket.

directions   During introductory activities, show the children the big container of peanut butter, the small coffee scoop, and the empty container. Ask: "How many scoops of peanut butter do you think it would take me to fill up this yogurt cup?" Write down the children's predictions on a chart if you like. Also, you can put one scoop of peanut butter in the container if you like, and show them how much space it occupies. Say: "If you'd like to find out how many scoops of peanut butter you'll need to fill up this cup, then everything you need to do that will be in the sensory table today." Show the kids the "One Person May Be Here" sign and ask them what it means. Also, show them the writing sheets and pens, and let them know that if they like, they can write down the number of scoops. Point out the soapy water and paper towels, and discuss their purpose. A nice follow up activity is to gather again at the end of the day, and talk about the activity, and have the kids tell you how many scoops it took them. Then have the children count the scoops as you fill up the cup. Compare that number with the numbers the children said, and compare whether it took more scoops or fewer scoops this time.

MATH/SOCIAL STUDIES:
Peanut Butter Balls

objective Facilitate comparison of cup measurements; facilitate rational counting; utilize fraction measurements; emphasize the concept of sharing.

materials
Peanut butter
Honey
Goodies: mixed raisins, coconut flakes, apple chips, carob chips, or other similar items
Plastic bowls — one for each child
A favorite cereal — Rice Crispies works especially well
One-third cup measuring cup
One-half cup measuring cup
One tablespoon
Wax paper squares
Masking tape
A marker
Popsicle sticks
A tub of soapy water
Paper towels
Picture sign showing ingredients and amounts:
1/3 cup peanut butter; 1/2 cup Rice Crispies;
3 big spoons goodies, above; and 2 big spoons honey

preparation Set the peanut butter, honey, mixed raisins etc., and cereal each in a large bowl, and set them around a small round table, with the appropriate sign next to each bowl. Have each child wash his/her hands before approaching the table. During the morning's introductory activities, ask the children if they've ever shared anything with someone. As they answer, ask: "How did so and so like it when you shared that? How did that make you feel?" After the children have commented, tell them that today you are all going to make one peanut butter ball for yourselves, and one to give someone else. Ask the kids for ideas about who they could give their other peanut butter ball to: a friend? Someone in their families? A relative?

directions Invite the children to take each ingredient from around the table. Help them read/interpret the sign, and encourage them to count out loud as they take the amount indicated by the sign. You'll probably have to help them scoop the peanut butter and honey out of the measuring cups, or show them how to do it. Encourage them to mix the ingredients with the popsicle sticks, and to then divide the peanut butter ball in half. Give them the wax paper to wrap their gift in, and ask them who they want to give it to. Write that person's name on masking tape, and let the children put their gifts on a tray in the refrigerator, to stay chilled until it's time to take them home or give them away. After the children have given their gifts, ask them about their experiences. Who did they give them to? What did those people say? How did the kids feel about it?

ART/SENSORY:
Peanut Butter Art

objective Facilitate creative expression; develop fine motor skills; facilitate a sensory experience using an unusual material; facilitate cooperative, group art experience.

materials
  Peanut butter
  Water
  Large piece of butcher paper
  Shallow pans

preparation In this activity, the children are going to hand and finger paint with peanut butter paint. Spread newspaper out on your work surface. Thin the peanut butter out with water until it's the consistency of paint that is suitable for hand painting. Cut the butcher paper out in the shape of a giant, unshelled peanut. Put the peanut butter paint in the shallow pans, and put them in the middle of the giant peanut, within easy reach of all children.

directions Stand back and watch! Ask the children to guess what the paint is made of. They may want to smell it for a clue. Use crunchy peanut butter, if you like, for an interesting variation.

ART:
Backwards Peanut Collage

objective Develop fine motor skills; develop self-esteem by having children help in preparation process.

materials
  Shirt boxes — six to eight for one large activity table
  Glue
  Peanut shells saved from other activities
  Pieces of paper that fit into the shirt boxes
  Glue brushes
  Yellow or light brown construction paper

preparation   Cut peanut shapes out of the construction paper. Have the children help you tear up the peanut shells into smaller pieces, or put them in zip lock bags and have the children stamp on them. If you break them down like this, ask the children if they can hear any crunching sounds. When the shells are broken up, keep them on hand. (They should be broken up into fairly fine pieces. If they are too fibrous to do this, roast them in the oven for a few minutes, to make them easier to break up.) Spread all materials out on the table. Sprinkle enough peanut shells to lightly cover all of the inside of the shirt boxes. Make a sample peanut picture by covering your peanut paper with glue, and dropping it, glue side down, onto the peanut shells in the box. Lift it out carefully and let it dry.

directions   Show the children your peanut picture during introductory activities, and tell the children about the different steps you followed to make it. An interesting variation in this activity is to color the glue with tempera paint.

GROSS MOTOR:
Squirrel Peanut Hunt

objective   Develop large motor muscles; stimulate cognitive skills through searching for hiding places.

materials   Peanuts
If possible, photographs of squirrels (See literature list below for some good books on squirrels.)
Small zip lock sandwich bags
Children's mallets

preparation   Either indoors or outdoors, depending on the weather and the number of good hiding places, hide peanuts in all kinds of interesting places.

directions   Ask the children if they've ever seen a squirrel. Show them your photographs, and tell them that squirrels like to eat nuts. Tell the children that you've hidden some peanuts, and suggest that you all pretend to be squirrels who are looking for nuts. Show the kids the limits within which the peanuts are hidden, and give them paper bags for what they find. Have extra peanuts available for kids who have a hard time discovering them. Tell the children that you are going to crush your peanuts before you eat them. After the hunt is over, sit together and make an activity out of shelling and crushing the peanuts. Also, it's important that the children sit down while they eat.

EXTENDING THE CONCEPT

math After your taste test, make a graph of how many children liked each kind of peanut. Younger children may not understand about voting only once, so let them vote for as many different kinds as they like, and then make a graph. With older children, ask them which kind was their favorite, and make a graph of that. Draw the outline for each column on the graph, and then ask them what color each column should be. Then let them color the columns. Older kids may also want to write or copy the words of the headings for each column.

language A story box is a box which contains a collection of miniature objects that are related to a poem or story. The poem or story is included in the box. A child manipulates the materials to retell the original story, and to create new ones. If you have a toy train set, make story boxes out of the peanut song. For this story box, provide a real unshelled peanut with a face drawn or glued onto it. Draw a blob of peanut butter on paper, and cover it with contact paper on both sides. Put these things in a box with some train track and a toy train engine. Write the words to the song on paper using pictures, and include it in the story box. For good measure, include a small bag of crushed peanuts for eating.

art/math From tagboard, cut out a giant peanut. Put out unshelled peanuts and glue, and cover the tagboard peanut by gluing real peanuts onto it. After the glue has dried, count the number of peanuts you all glued on, and write the number on the tagboard.

LITERATURE

*Selsam, Millicent E., *Peanut*, Morrow Jr. Books
Keller, Charles, *The Nutty Joke Book*, Prentice-Hall Inc., 1978
Ryden, Hope, *The Raggedy Red Squirrel*, Lodestar Books, 1992
Van Warmer, Joe, *Squirrels*, E.P. Dutton, 1978
McConoughey, Jana, *The Squirrels*, Crestwood House, 1983
(Good photographs in all the above squirrel books.)

Suck a lemon
tart and sour;
boy, that fruit
has pucker power!

THEME: lemons

My co-teacher and I had a blast with this theme, primarily because the lemonade stand is so much fun. If you're stuck for something to use as a stand, do what we did, and get a refrigerator box from a furniture store. Cut out a door and a window, put a small table inside, and voila! — you're in business. Making lemonade is an obvious activity for this theme, so I tried to suggest other, more unusual projects for the unit.

INTRODUCTORY ACTIVITIES

ATTENTION GRABBER

Cut a lemon into enough slices for each child to have one, as well as one spare slice. Put the slices in a bowl, and when the kids have gathered, ask them to close their eyes and to guess what they're smelling. Take the spare slice, and pass it under their noses. If or when the kids guess what it is, let each one take a slice to taste. Suggest that they take a very small taste at first. After the initial taste, you may want to have some sugar handy, to sprinkle on the slices, or you may not. Ask the kids about their experience.

INTRODUCTORY DISCUSSION

objective   Introduce the theme; stimulate language development; expand vocabulary.

materials   Lemon rhyme

directions   Read the rhyme at least twice. Talk with the children about what the words tart, sour, and pucker mean. Having tasted a lemon slice in the attention grabber activity, these words will have more meaning for them. Ask the children what their mouths did when they tasted the lemon. What does it feel like when your mouth puckers? Ask the children what else is sour. Ask them if they've ever eaten food with lemons in it.

GROSS MOTOR/SOCIAL STUDIES:
No-Hands Lemon Pass

objective   Develop problem solving skills; develop muscle control; facilitate experimentation with unusual ways of passing an item; help children see the benefits of cooperation.

materials   A lemon
Masking tape

preparation   Make a masking tape circle and place cross marks about 2 1/2 to 3 feet away from each other, all around the circle.

directions   Ask the kids to find a cross mark to sit on. Tell them that you're all going to pass or roll the lemon around the circle to each other, and that there's only one rule: no one can use hands. Brainstorm with the kids to think about what other parts of your bodies you might be able to use to pass or roll the lemon: elbows, feet, legs, head? Then start the game. Almost always, the child to whom the lemon is being passed will instinctively reach out with a part of her/his body to help the one who is doing the passing. After playing this game for a while, tell them how you noticed them helping each other this way. Tell the kids you're going to try passing the lemon to the wall. After they watch you try this (and after they've giggled at you), ask them why it would have been easier to pass the lemon to one of them.

MUSIC/MOVEMENT:
Old Goat Tucker

objective   Develop cognition through memorization of words; develop cognitive skills by remembering associated actions; help children enjoy singing.

materials

To the tune of Turkey In The Straw:
Once there was a goat named old goat Tucker;
she was hungry so she went and poked around in the cupboard.
Well, she found one lemon in the back of the shelf
and she gobbled it up all by herself.
Gobbled it up, gobbled it up,
that sour old lemon in the back of the shelf,
she gobbled it up all by herself.

Well, oh too bad for old goat Tucker,
'cause boy, did that lemon make her poor mouth pucker.
Her mistress came along and said: "I see you've devoured
that lemon on the shelf that was old and sour."
Mistress came along, Mistress came along,
Mistress came to say: "I see you've devoured
that lemon on the shelf that was old and sour."

Well old goat Tucker shook and shook her head
to shake that taste right out of her head.
Mistress said, "Drink some water and you'll be all right."
But the mouth of the goat was puckered all night.
If you eat a lemon, watch out!

directions

For "There was a goat named old goat Tucker," get down on all fours and butt your head. For "She was hungry and went to poke around in the cupboard," pretend to poke your head around in a cupboard and sniff for food. For "She found a lemon in the back of the shelf and she gobbled it up all by herself," move your mouth in large, slow chews. Repeat for chorus. For "But oh, too bad for old goat Tucker," shake your pointer finger. For " 'cause boy did that lemon make her poor mouth pucker," wince and suck your cheeks in. For "Her mistress came along," put your hands on both hips For "I see you've devoured that lemon on the shelf that was old and sour," shake your pointer finger. Repeat for chorus. For "Old goat Tucker shook and shook her head," shake your head. Do so even harder for "to shake that taste right out of her head." For "Mistress said, 'Drink some water and you'll be all right,'" pretend to drink some water. For "But the mouth of the goat was puckered all night!", point to your mouth and pucker it again. For "If you eat a lemon, watch out!", pretend to hold a lemon in your hand and give the warning with an earnest expression on your face. With younger children, you may want to teach only one or two verses, or spend several days helping the kids learn one verse before you teach the children the next.

ACTIVITY CENTERS

LANGUAGE:
Old Goat Tucker Flannel Board Story

objective
Develop cognitive skills by encouraging kids to recall and tell the story; develop imagination by encouraging them to create their own stories.

materials
Old Goat Tucker flannel board story on page NOTE
Flannel board figures (Clip art section, page NOTE)
A flannel board
A "Two People May Be Here" sign

preparation
Make the flannel board using the figures pages NOTE. For cupboard, cut door flaps in a square flannel piece.

directions
After you've sung the song without the flannel board for a few mornings, bring out the flannel board story and sing it while you use the pieces. Let the kids know that the flannel board and pieces will be set out at a table during free play.

ART:
Lemon Sprinkle

objective
Develop fine motor skills through sprinkling; facilitate creative expression; provide the opportunity to explore unconventional art materials.

materials
Lemon pepper seasoning
Empty plastic spice bottles with sprinkle tops
Glue
Glue brushes
Paper
Newspaper

preparation Spread newspaper out on your work surface. Divide the lemon pepper among the empty spice containers. If you like, cut your paper in the shape of lemons. Put the rest of the materials out on the table. Put the lemon pepper seasoning bottles in the middle of the table. If you have time, grate the rinds off lemons you'll be using to make lemonade in the Social Studies/Science activity (Extending the Concept) below, and add the gratings to the lemon pepper. Make a lemon sprinkle picture yourself.

directions During introductory activities, show the children your lemon sprinkle picture and tell the kids how you made it. Let them smell the picture. Point out the materials on the table. As the children put glue on their paper and sprinkle the lemon pepper on it, invite them to smell the seasoning. Ask if they can smell the lemon in it.

ART:
Lemon Roll

objective Develop muscle control; facilitate experimentation with unusual art materials.

materials Shirt boxes (lids aren't needed)
Small lemons
Paper
Paint
Large spoons

preparation Spread newspaper out on your work surface. Arrange all materials on the table. Put a piece of paper inside a box, a few spoonfuls of paint, and put a lemon inside. Roll the lemon around until the paint is spread on the paper, and leave the box with the paper and lemon in it in the middle of the table as a sample.

directions Invite the kids to make their own lemon roll pictures.

SCIENCE:
Lemon And Ball Comparison

objective Facilitate scientific comparison of how a lemon rolls as compared to a ball; stimulate curiosity.

materials   All materials of Lemon Roll activity above
Balls that are roughly the same size as the lemons

directions   After the children have
had a chance to make
lemon roll pictures,
put out the balls.
If/when the children
use the balls to make
pictures, ask them which
rolls more smoothly,
easily, or quickly — the lemon
or the ball? Encourage the kids to
look closely at the shape of each and
to compare them, as well as to verbalize
observations and hypotheses about why they roll differently.

MATH/SENSORY:
Lemon Water Measuring

objective   Facilitate measuring with measuring cups; provide sensory experience with
pouring and with lemon slices.

materials   Measuring cups
Yellow food coloring
Tubs or a sensory table
Lemons
Water

preparation   Put water and the measuring cups in a sensory table or tubs. Add yellow food
coloring. Cut some lemons into slices, and some into wedges. Leave a few
whole lemons intact, and add all the fruit to the water.

directions   Stand back and enjoy the children's exploration of these materials.

DRAMATIC PLAY:
Lemonade Stand

objective   Help children connect words with actions; help kids imagine situations;
develop conversational skills; facilitate child-to-child interactions.

materials
A refrigerator box and/or a table
Large bowls
Lemonade made from frozen concentrate
Lemon slices
Ladles
Cash registers
Coins
Children's aprons
Paper cups
A small table
Chairs
A table cloth
A small plastic vase with
   flowers, real or plastic
A sign for the lemonade
   stand

preparation Set up the lemon stand with the bowls of lemonade, ladles, cups, cash registers and paper cups on the table. Spread the table cloth on the table, put the vase and flowers in the middle, and place a few chairs next to it. Before the kids play with the materials, you may want to reinforce how important it is to cover one's mouth when coughing or sneezing, and also, to sit down when drinking.

directions Take some coins and buy a cup of lemonade.

EXTENDING THE CONCEPT

social studies/ science Make lemonade, and encourage each child to squeeze the juice out of a lemon using a hand squeezer or electric squeezer. When all the children have made some juice, compare the total amount to the juice of one lemon. Ask the children: "Do you think there would have been enough lemonade for all of us if we only had the juice that one person squeezed?" Tell the kids you're glad that everyone helped make lemonade for each other. Let the children add teaspoons of sugar to the lemon juice. Experiment. What does the lemonade taste like right after the sugar has been added? What does it taste like after the sugar's been stirred in? There should be enough for everyone to have a little cupful, but have some lemon juice concentrate on hand in case you have to stretch it out. _

science After rolling lemons and balls for art in the art activity, experiment with rolling balls and lemons down ramps. Do they roll differently? Does one seem to roll faster or straighter than another? Why?

math Put a number of lemon slices in a bowl next to a sign that says 'Would you like to count the lemon slices?'

sensory Ahead of time, ask friends, relatives or neighbors to help you collect the kind of plastic lemons that lemon juice concentrate is sometimes packaged in. Put these in water and let the kids play with them.

LITERATURE

Jeunesse, Gallimard, *Fruit*, Scholastic, 1989
Mitgutsch, Ali, *From Lemon To Lemonade*, CarolRhoda Books, 1986
*Asch, Frank, *Good Lemonade*, Franklin Watts, 1976 (Except for quite sexist text and illustration on the eighth page — girls in bikinis used to sell lemonade — this is a good story. I usually skip this page when I read the book, although another approach is to include and discuss it. I find the issue it raises to be too complicated for the very young kids I teach, but you'll know whether or not it's appropriate to discuss with your group.)

Oodles of noodles

do slither so slippery,

gliding and sliding

in piles so slickery.

THEME: noodles

This is another one of those food items which lends itself perfectly to a large variety of natural learning activities. The huge diversity in pasta shapes and sizes is ideal for math activities, and my children have spent quite long periods of time at the sensory table scooping, weighing, and bagging noodles. Most kids I know love to eat spaghetti, so that's another point of reference. I've suggested making your own pasta noodles as an extender activity only because you may not have a pasta maker — but if you have one, I'd suggest making this a primary activity.

INTRODUCTORY ACTIVITIES

ATTENTION GRABBER

Cook up some rice noodles ahead of time, and when the children are gathered, ask them to close their eyes and put out their hands. Tell them that the thing you're going to put in their hand is something they can eat, and will give them a clue about what you'll be talking about all week. (My local supermarket had quite a good selection of Asian noodle varieties, including rice and bean thread noodles. Hopefully, for convenience, yours does too.)

INTRODUCTORY DISCUSSION/SOCIAL STUDIES

objective Introduce theme; develop speaking and listening skills; introduce the concept that the same food has a different shape and name in different cultures, and can be made from wheat, bean or rice.

materials
Noodle rhyme
Cooked and dry spaghetti noodles
Cooked and dry Udon (Japanese noodles)
Cooked and dry Quatial (Thai rice noodles)
Cooked and dry bean thread noodles
Chow Mein noodles
A few beans
A little flour
A little rice

directions Read the rhyme at least twice. Ask the kids if they eat noodles at home. What shape are the noodles they eat? Do they eat anything with the noodles? You should decide how to introduce the following information depending on the age of your kids. With younger children, you may want to introduce one noodle and its source a day at a time over the duration of the unit. Older children can probably absorb more information at one session. The noodle types listed in the Materials list above are really based on the varieties my supermarket carries — you may end up with different samples. The important thing is to try to get a variety of noodles from diverse cultures. As you introduce each kind of noodle, be sure to also show the kids your source samples (flour, rice, beans). Talk to the children about the different names of noodles. Japanese noodles are called udon. Italian noodles are called pasta. They're both made from flour which comes from wheat. Quatial (Kway tee ow), or rice noodles, are made from rice. Bean thread noodles are made from beans. Crunchy Chinese noodles are called chow mein noodles. As you learn

the noodle names, tap them on your knees, noses, the floor, or any other interesting place that will help you remember them. Pass a few of each kind of noodle around. You may decide to have cooked samples for the kids to taste. How are they different? Put all raw samples on a table for examination during free play.

MUSIC/GROSS MOTOR:
Noodle Dance

objective Develop cognition by remembering words and connected actions; exercise large muscles; help children enjoy singing.

materials To the tune of Here We Are Together, sing:
Did you ever see a noodle, a noodle, a noodle,
did you ever see a noodle, go this way and that?
It flips and it flops and it slithers and it slides.
Did you ever see a noodle go this way and that?

directions For "Did you ever," put both your hands out in a questioning gesture. For "see," point to both eyes. For "noodle," make your mouth make as much of an "ooo" sound as possible. For "go this way and that," put both hands on your hips and bend from side to side. For "It flips," bend forward; for "it flops," bend backwards; for "it slithers and it slides," make your arms slither and slide. Vary the way you sing it — sing it very slowly, very fast, and lastly, by trying to remember to skip the word "noodle."

ACTIVITY CENTERS

MATH:
Noodle Match/Noodle Count

objective Facilitate one-on-one matching for young children; facilitate rational counting and/or subtraction for older children; develop reading, speaking and listening skills.

materials   A variety of pasta noodles diverse in shape and size —
lasagna, elbow, manicotti, corkscrew, wheels, etc.
Containers
Tagboard
Markers
Pens
Puppet
Picture sign saying, "Would you like to match the noodles?"
Subtraction signs (described below)

preparation   For a simple matching game, spread noodles diverse in size and shape across
all areas of a blank piece of tagboard. Trace their outlines with a black
marker. Write the name of each noodle underneath the outline using
printscript or D'Nealian. Put the actual noodles on a tray next to the tagboard
chart, either on a table or a safe place on the floor. (Have extras of each
noodle in case some get broken.) Hang the picture sign above the materials,
and place blank writing sheets and pens nearby. I've found that older children
also enjoy matching games, but whiz through them at record speed. For a
more challenging activity, sort some of each kind of noodle into separate
containers. Choose the amount of each noodle according to how high your
kids count. Label each container by gluing onto the lid a sample of the noodle
contained inside. Make a subtraction sign for each kind of noodle by writing
"Take __ noodles away. How many left?" Replace the blank with the number
of that kind of noodle you want them to subtract. Glue that number of
noodles over the words. (The noodles you glue onto the cards should
correspond with the ones in the containers.) Each container should have a
subtraction sign.

directions   While the children explore the materials, take your puppet out, and using the
puppet's personality, ask the kids what they're doing.

MATH:
Noodle Measure

objective   Facilitate an understanding of what measuring is; facilitate an understanding
that any uniform object can be used to measure; facilitate rational counting;
develop all components of language: speaking, listening, reading and writing.

materials   Two, three or four boxes of lasagna noodles
Markers
Butcher paper

preparation   Have all materials available. You're going to be making body maps on the
butcher paper, so you may want to have pre-torn sheets available. You'll also
need one large enough for your own body. Save the lasagna noodles after this
project to use for the noodle brush activity below.

directions When you see some children at loose ends or in between activities, lay down on the butcher paper, and ask the kids if anyone would like to take a marker and trace around your body. When this is done, ask the kids if they would measure your body with lasagna noodles. Sit up and begin laying the noodles end to end, parallel to your leg, to give the children the idea. When they've finished laying the noodles down, tell them you're going to count them now to see how many lasagna noodles tall you are. Invite them to count with you. When you know the answer, trace a lasagna noodle next to the outline of your body, and next to it, write the number it took to measure you. Then write out an entire sentence: "I used __ lasagna noodles to measure my body." Ask the kids if they would like to have their own body measure. Usually other children are willing and anxious to trace around their friends and to lay out the noodles next to them. Take dictation, or encourage the kids to write their own sentences about how many noodles it took to measure their outlines. When the body measures are done, put them up on the walls. During the next day's introductory activities, ask if anyone would like to point out their body measure and tell the group about it.

ART:
Pasta Pots

objective Develop creative expression; develop fine motor skills; provide art experience with unusual materials.

materials Black construction paper
White paper
Cooked spaghetti noodles, some colored with food coloring
Glue
Glue brushes

preparation Cut pasta pot outlines out of the black construction paper. When you cook the spaghetti, add food coloring to the boiling water for colored spaghetti if you like, making several differently colored batches of noodles. Or, you may prefer to leave all your noodles uncolored. (At the same time as you prepare these noodles, you may want to cook enough noodles for the Noodle-Rama activity below.) Spread newspaper out on your work surface, and arrange all materials on top.

directions During the morning's introductory activities, read *Strega Nona* by Tomie De Paola. After the story, let the children know that they can make their own pasta pot pictures if they like. Some children prefer to skip the pasta pot and instead make creative pictures by gluing colored spaghetti onto paper. Other kids really "get into" the pasta pot pictures, gluing huge mounds of overflowing pasta on their pots.

ART:
Noodle Brushes

objective Develop artistic imagination; provide experience with using an unusual art utensil.

materials Two or three lasagna noodles (left over from body measure activity above)
Two or three containers of paint
Paper
Boiling water

preparation Spread newspaper out on your work surface. Microwave or boil some water, and put it in a mug. Dip about three quarters of an inch of each lasagna noodle into the hot water to soften the end and create a brush. If you soften too much of the noodle, the soft part will break off while the kids use it, so three quarters of an inch is the most you want to soften. Put the noodle brushes in the containers of paint, and put paper on the table, too.

directions Encourage the children to use the noodle brushes.

SENSORY:
Noodle-Rama

objective Provide sensory experience with cooked noodles; heighten awareness of sense of touch.

materials Cooked noodles, colored with food coloring if desired
A sensory table or plastic tubs
A pasta server if possible
Plastic strawberry baskets
Containers
Forks

preparation Put noodles, pasta server, strawberry baskets, containers and forks in the tubs or sensory table.

directions During the day's introductory activities, ask the children if they think it would be O.K. to eat the noodles in the sensory table. Usually kids say no. If you hear a yes, explain that your fingers have germs on them, and the noodles will have lots of germs on them, too. Even with very young children, I don't often have a problem with this — the kids seem to instinctively know the difference between food to eat and food to play with. Still, it's worth mentioning.

SCIENCE: Noodle Mold

objective Facilitate first hand observation and knowledge of molds; facilitate observing, hypothesizing, discovering, and concluding; develop all components of language: speaking, listening, reading and writing.

materials
Plastic zip lock baggies
Cooked spaghetti noodles
Vegetable oil
Small container
Spoon
Tagboard chart for observations (described below)
Pens or marker
Duct tape
Masking tape

preparation Have enough cooked noodles available for each child to put some in his/her baggie. Put a masking tape label on every bag so that you can easily write each child's name on it. Put some noodles in one bag, zip it closed, and write your name on the bag. Write an observation about your noodles on the chart. Have all the rest of the materials available on an activity table, and a space on the wall on which the baggies can be taped. If the baggies are too close to sunlight, the moisture needed for mold will be absent. There are two ways of developing writing and reading skills in this activity: for young children (3s and 4s), you may prefer to put up only the tagboard chart. For older children, you may want to have each make an observation book by folding a few sheets of paper in half and stapling on the fold. This way, each child can record his or her observations, and time can be put aside for sharing the observations at the end of each day. If you're using a chart, put it up on the wall near the assigned noodle bag spot. Otherwise, put the blank observation books with pens on a table near the experiment.

directions During the day's introductory activities, talk to the children about mold. Let them know that there are very small specks like dust that float in the air, and that they're called "spores." Spores like to grow on moist, warm foods and they make molds. Ask the kids if they've ever seen mold. Sadly, I've been unable to find any books on mold, but you may have better luck. If so, it's ideal to have photographs of mold on hand. Show the children your noodle bag, and tape it to the wall. Tell the kids you're going to leave it for a while to see if it grows mold. Tell them you're going to observe it every day, and write down what you notice. Read them your observation for that day. Tell the kids that everything they need for their own noodle mold experiment is on one of the activity tables. During free play, when the children approach the table and put some noodles in their bags, ask them if they'd like to put a little oil in the noodles, too. This is extra food for the spores. (If all the kids choose to put oil in their bags, make a few noodle bags yourself, without oil, so that you can compare the results.) Write each child's name on an observation book, and leave the books and pens on a table near the bags. If you're using a chart, take story dictation every day, and read their observations back to them. With older 4s and young 5s, I've often written down their words on separate paper because they like to copy the words down on the chart themselves. If you're using observation books, you can either take dictation, write down the words for copying, or help your kids write their words directly into their books. You'll know which method best suits your kids. After mold begins to show, invite the children to show and tell about their noodles and observation books, or to 'read' from the chart during introductory activities.

LANGUAGE:
On Top Of Spaghetti Flannel Board/Picture Chart Center

objective   Develop all components of language arts: speaking, listening, reading, writing; develop vocabulary; facilitate creativity with language; stimulate imagination.

materials   Flannel Board
Felt, any color
Magazines, particularly homemaking or food magazines
Scissors
Clear contact paper
Pale construction paper
Butcher paper or tagboard
Glue sticks
Cooked spaghetti
Pens
A "Two People May Be Here" sign
Two tables; one a small, two-person work surface

Song:
On top of spaghetti, all covered with cheese,
I lost my poor meatball, when somebody sneezed.

It rolled off of the table, and onto the floor,
and then my poor meatball, rolled right out the door.

It rolled into garden, and under a bush.
And then my poor meatball was nothing but mush.

preparation Make a flannel board story and a picture chart of the above song. You can cut out from magazines two pictures of each item. (I was surprised how many photos of meatballs and spaghetti there are in food magazines — they weren't hard to find at all.) Look through food, furniture, and homemaking magazines to find photographs of a meatball, spaghetti noodles, a door, a table, grass or a garden, and a bush. Before you cut any pieces out, use a large piece of clear contact paper to cover the photographs. Then cut two pictures of each item out and glue one of each onto a large piece of felt. Make a picture chart by writing the words to the song on either butcher paper or tagboard, and gluing the second set of pictures above the words. You can also glue cooked spaghetti onto the chart for the noodles. They'll dry and add an interesting dimension to the chart. Put the chart up on a wall, and next to it, place the larger table and chairs. On this table, put construction paper, magazines, scissors, pens, glue sticks, and cooked spaghetti. At the two-person table, place the flannel board and flannel pieces, and prominently display the "Two People May Be Here" sign.

directions During the morning's introductory activities, sing the meatball song, using the flannel board pieces while you do. If you like, have the children take turns putting the flannel board pieces on the board while the rest of you sing the song. Let the kids know that the flannel board will be available for them to play with during the morning. Sing the song once again, this time using the picture chart. Ask the kids what they see above the word 'spaghetti.' They'll recognize the real noodles. Show them the construction paper, pens, glue sticks and markers on the table below the picture chart, and let them know they can make their own chart of the song if they like. Older children often copy the words they see, and younger children like to glue noodles and make scribble sentences.

LANGUAGE/DRAMATIC PLAY/MATH:
Pasta Shop

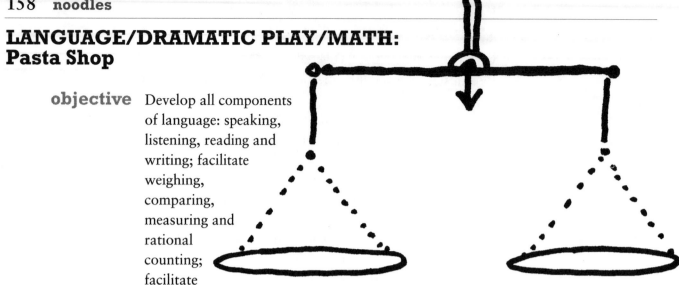

objective   Develop all components of language: speaking, listening, reading and writing; facilitate weighing, comparing, measuring and rational counting; facilitate

acting out of real life situations (shopping); facilitate child-to-child interactions.

materials

Several bags of uncooked noodles — enough to provide a substantial amount for scooping and weighing.

Balancing scales

Sensory table or tubs

Toy cash registers

Scoops, spoons and containers

Paper lunch bags cut down to be about 5" high to facilitate easy filling

Simulated checkbooks (described below)

Pasta order forms (described below)

Pens

Telephone

Pennies or nickels

Sign for pasta shop

Photographs of noodles from food magazines

preparation   To make checkbooks, enlarge and photocopy a blank check (with account number blacked out, if you feel it's necessary) several times for each child. Cut out the checks and staple into books for each child. For pasta order forms, fold a piece or 8 1/2 x 11 paper in quarters, and in each quarter, write: "Pasta Order Form," and draw three or four lines with a ruler under the header. Photocopy and cut out along the fold lines. Set out all materials to simulate a pasta shop. Put the spoons, scoops, and containers in the tubs with the dry pasta. Set out the cash registers, checkbooks, order forms, pens and telephone on a long table to simulate a store counter. Put the photographs on the walls around the pasta shop, and also, the sign for the pasta shop in a prominent place. Place the paper bags near the weighing scales, which should be near the sensory table of noodles.

directions   Take some nickels or pennies, and tell the shop proprietors you need some special noodles for a macaroni salad you're making for a party (or other pasta needs!)

EXTENDING THE CONCEPT

art When you make noodle pictures, a fun variation is to provide cooked noodles and paper without glue. The noodles will stick to paper by themselves.

art/fine motor/ math Use rubbing alcohol and food coloring in sealed plastic bags to color uncooked macaroni noodles. Leave them out to dry, and roll masking tape around the ends of string lengths for easy threading. Then let the kids make macaroni necklaces. Make extra colored noodles for sorting.

science When you experiment with the noodle mold activity, another variation is to poke air holes in some of the bags. Do the bags with air holes produce different molds?

science/math If you can borrow a pasta maker, or find an inexpensive one at a garage sale, it's great fun to make your own pasta noodles. With the children, add garlic powder, oregano, and basil to canned tomato sauce, heat it up, and put it on top of your spaghetti. Grated cheese is also a nice extra touch.

math Place one of each of a variety of noodles that are seriated in size on a tray which says: "Would you like to sort the noodles from biggest to smallest?"

LITERATURE

Haycock, Kate, *Pasta*, CarolRhoda Books, 1989
*Machotka, Hana, *Pasta Factory*, Houghton Mifflin Company, 1992 (Terrific photographs. There's a lot of text, so you may want to talk the kids through the book, or read selectively.)
de Paola, Tomie, *Strega Nona*, Scholastic Inc., 1975
Barret, Judi, *Cloudy With A Chance Of Meatballs*, Scholastic Inc., 1978

Crick, crack,

broken open,

out they ooze,

those yellow

yolken.

THEME: eggs

Eggs can contain bacteria, so during the sensory activity it's a good idea to provide soapy water for hand washing afterwards. I've never had a problem with children contracting a disease or becoming ill from this activity. You'll probably want to start saving and collecting eggshells well in advance of teaching this unit. Rinse them out thoroughly and let them dry before you use them.

INTRODUCTORY ACTIVITIES

ATTENTION GRABBER

Ahead of time, hard-boil an egg. Put it in a feely box (cut a knee-high nylon or sock at the ankle and stretch the other end around the opening of an oatmeal container, so that children can put their hands in the sock and feel the item without being able to see it) or a paper bag. When the kids are gathered, pass

the box or bag around and invite them to feel what's inside. Can they guess what it is? Take the egg out when everyone has had a chance to feel and guess, and ask what the children think you'll be talking about this week.

INTRODUCTORY DISCUSSION

objective   Introduce the theme; stimulate language use; develop listening skills; expand vocabulary.

materials   Egg rhyme

directions   Read the rhyme at least twice. Ask the children if they've ever broken an egg open. What was inside? What did it feel like? What did they do with the egg? What kinds of things ooze? What color are yolks? What color is the rest of a raw egg? Ask the children if they ever use made-up words. Ask the kids to listen for a made-up word in the rhyme, and read it again. Close your eyes and pretend to break an egg on your heads while you say the egg rhyme.

MUSIC/MOVEMENT:
Six Little Eggs

objective   Help children have fun singing; facilitate understanding of the concept of subtraction; develop cognition by memorizing words and associated movements.

materials   To the tune of Five Little Ducks:
Six little eggs were sitting in a carton;
One rolled away to play in the garden.
The others called, "Oh please come back!"
But all they heard was a mighty crack.
Five little eggs...(and so on)

Optional: Six plastic eggs
A six-cup egg carton
Circular light-colored stickers; one for each egg

directions   If you're doing this as a finger play without the plastic eggs and carton, you can perform the following motions: for "Six little eggs sitting in a carton," hold up six fingers. For "One rolled away to play in the garden," hold up your pointer finger for "one," and then roll your hands around each other to simulate tumbling. For "The others called, 'Oh please come back!'" put your hands to your mouth. For "But all they heard was a mighty crack," put one hand to your ear in a listening gesture for "all they heard," and make a wincing expression with your face for "mighty crack." If you're singing the song with plastic eggs, take one egg away for each verse, and then let the children take turns with the plastic eggs while the rest of you sing the song. To prepare the plastic eggs, draw little faces on the circular stickers, and affix one to each egg.

SOCIAL STUDIES:
Who Are Vegans And Vegetarians?

objective   Help the children understand that some people don't eat meat, and that some other people don't eat meat, milk, cheese or eggs.

directions   After you've sung the above song, and before you disperse for free play, ask the children whether they know that some people don't eat meat. Tell them that people who don't eat meat are called "vegetarians." To reinforce the word, say: "Let's tap that word on the floor, on our noses, on our knees," and so forth, and use your finger to tap with, while you say the word. With very young children, talk about the word vegetarian again during several introductory sessions before you introduce the word "vegan." When you discuss this word, tell the children that some people don't eat meat or eggs or milk or cheese. Those people are called vegans. One of the books listed under Literature, *Eggs*, by Dorothy Turner, raises the issue of factory farming. This is a good book to use if the children wonder why some people don't eat eggs.

ACTIVITY CENTERS

SENSORY:
Egg Exploration

objective   Facilitate a sensory exploration of eggs; develop speaking, listening and reading skills.

materials   A tub of soapy water
Paper towels
An egg for each child, some eggs brown (available at health food stores) and some white.
A bowl for each place at the table
Chart paper
Markers — 2 different colors

preparation   Hang your blank chart paper up near the activity table. Place a bowl in front of each chair at the table, and put the eggs in the middle. Have the soapy water and towels nearby. If you feel comfortable with how clean the kids' hands are while they do this activity, and there aren't too many eggshells present, you can save the eggs for the Omelet Time below.

directions   Encourage the children to approach the table, break open an egg in their bowls, and feel the egg inside. As the children feel the eggs, ask them what they feel like, and write their comments on the chart, using D'Nealian or printscript, and alternating colors for each sentence. Use quotation marks, and write the speaker's name after his/her comment. After the activity, read the observations back to the children. Have the kids wash their hands after this activity.

GROSS MOTOR:
Egg Hunt

objective   Develop large muscle groups; develop cognition; develop fine motor skills.

materials   Enough hard-boiled eggs for each child to have one

preparation   Hide the hard-boiled eggs in interesting hiding places.

directions   Let the children know that when they find an egg, they must sit down to eat it, and let other children hunt for the rest. If you like, have some salt and pepper available for dipping. If the children need help peeling the eggs, assist them. Save the eggshells for the Eggshell Collage below.

ART:
Eggshell Collage

objective Facilitate creative expression; develop fine motor skills; facilitate experimentation with interesting collage materials.

materials Eggshells, rinsed and dried (from Egg Hunt activity above)
Paper
Glitter
Glitter shakers
Glue
Glue brushes

preparation Spread newspaper out over your work surface. Arrange all materials on the table such that they are accessible to all children. If you like, cut your paper into egg shapes.

directions Stand back and enjoy the children's exploration of the materials.

ART:
Egg Carton Nature Boxes/Part 1

objective Facilitate creative expression and develop fine motor skills.

materials Cardboard egg cartons
Paint
Paint brushes
Glue
Crepe paper cut into confetti
Glitter
Yarn
Buttons
Interesting papers/tin foils cut into pieces
Paper curlicues

preparation If you're working with younger children (3's and 4's), you'll probably want to cut your egg cartons in half so that your kids only have 6 sections to fill. Cover your work surface with newspaper, and arrange all materials so that they're accessible to all children. Using the materials, decorate the outside of your own egg carton container first, and then, using the materials in part 2 below, put an interesting object of your choice in each egg carton section. You can either glue the object in, or leave it loose, depending on which you'd prefer. If you glue the objects, no part of your exhibit will get lost, but if the objects are loose, they can be taken out and examined. Write about and/or name each object on sticky labels, and affix to the inside of the lid. Number

your exhibits, and write the corresponding number on the inside of each egg carton section. Most children won't make their own nature boxes this formally, but sometimes a few children number a few of their sections, and your numbering will give them the idea.

directions   During the day's introductory activities, show the children your decorated egg carton nature box. With the kids, examine the outside of the box before you open it. Ask them what colors they notice, and what objects they see glued onto it. Then ask the kids to guess what's inside it. After everyone's had a chance to guess, open it and look inside. See part 2 for the remainder of the directions. After executing these, ask the kids if they'd like to make their own nature boxes. You'll have to do the decorating one day, let the boxes dry, and then fill the boxes the next day. Explain this to the children.

ART:
Egg Carton Nature Boxes/Part 2

objective   Develop self-esteem and sense of autonomy by providing the children with many decisions to make and materials to choose from; develop all components of language: speaking, listening, reading and writing skills.

materials   Decorated egg cartons from above activity
Interesting, small rocks or pebbles
Small pine cones
Acorns or other seeds or nuts
Interesting leaves
Small shells
Dead insects (optional for the squeamish!)
Small feathers
Any other nature objects you like
Glue
Brushes
Sticky labels
Pens
Markers

preparation   In looking over this list of nature objects, don't despair. My experience has been that the objects don't have to be very exotic to appeal to children. Usually they're thrilled just to have a large collection to choose from. I was able to collect quite an assortment of objects just by going on a few walks. The feathers of wild birds can carry diseases and can be hard to find. An easy way to get clean feathers is to call a pet store that has a good number of birds, explain your purpose, and ask if you can have some small feathers that the birds have molted. A friend or relation who owns birds might be another source. Arrange all the above materials on a table, and include the children's dried and decorated boxes.

directions   As suggested above, after having the children guess the contents of your box, open it up and let them examine your exhibit. Let them talk about each object. Show them how you numbered your exhibits, and read each name or description from your labels on the lid. Ask them if they'd like to make their own nature boxes, and let them know the materials are available on a table. When the kids become involved in creating their nature boxes, ask them if they'd like to write about their objects. Show them the labels and pens, and either take dictation or help them write their own words. Before the children take their nature boxes home or to their bedrooms, ask them, during the next day's introductory activities, if anyone would like to show and tell about their nature boxes. Ask them what they used to decorate the outside of the nature boxes in addition to asking about the contents. Since the materials used in this activity are nature objects found outside, it's a good idea to have the kids wash their hands afterwards. Also, before the activity, talk to them about the importance of keeping their fingers out of their mouths.

MATH:
Egg Match

objective   Provide one-to-one matching for young children; provide rational counting and subtracting experience for older children; develop cognition by identifying different colors; develop all components of language: speaking, listening, reading and speaking skills.

materials
2 sets of plastic eggshells, each set containing eggs of different colors (craft stores).
Small objects, perhaps manipulatives or sorting toys, that match the plastic eggshells in color.
Writing sheets (described below)
Pens
A two-person work table
"Two people may be here" sign

preparation   In this activity, you're going to find for each plastic egg small objects of the same color, for matching and counting, that you can put inside. For each set, fill some eggs with the corresponding colored object(s), but leave some eggs open and empty, with the contents loose on the table or tray. For young children, put only one object in each egg. For older children, put in several. Make and photocopy a writing sheet that asks, "How many (name of object) in the (color of egg) egg?" Have lines below the questions for children to record their answers. On the sheets, if you have time, color in the egg colors with crayons, or just put a scribble of the corresponding color on each egg. Put one set of eggs, writing sheets and pens at each place, so that two children will be working face to face. Although they won't do the math problems on the writing sheets, younger children may identify the matching egg colors and may enjoy scribbling in the space beneath them. I've discovered that a sign isn't necessary for this activity — the kids seem to know instinctively what to do with the eggs and their contents.

directions   Stand back and enjoy the children's exploration of the objects.

MATH/SCIENCE:
Omelet Time

objective   Facilitate measuring and counting exercise; facilitate observation of how heat changes the texture and form of eggs; develop self-esteem and sense of autonomy by enabling the kids to eat their own self-made snacks.

materials
Eggs
Milk
Margarine
A bowl of salt
Small plastic bowls — one for each child
Forks
A bowl of sliced mushrooms
A bowl of sliced green pepper
A bowl of sliced onions
A bowl of grated cheese
Spoons
Picture ingredient signs (described below)
Two tables, preferably round
An electric frying pan, if possible
Small plastic plates

preparation   Make a picture sign on an index card for each ingredient that shows the amount each child should take for his/her omelet. Set the eggs, milk, and salt around one table with corresponding signs indicating amounts to be used. Put

the vegetables and grated cheese around the other table. The children will be walking around the tables taking ingredients, so leave plenty of space around and between them. If you use an electric frying pan in the vicinity of the children, barricade it off with tables and chairs while it's heating.

directions Encourage the children to walk around the first table and follow each sign's directions. After they've scrambled their egg, milk and salt together with forks, invite the kids to walk around the second table and choose the vegetables they'd like for their omelet. The frying pan should be fairly hot, and the omelet should only take a few minutes to cook. Serve each cooked omelet to the child who assembled it, and encourage her/him to sit down and enjoy it.

LANGUAGE:
Picture Omelet Recipe Cards

objective Develop all components of language: speaking, listening, reading, writing.

materials Tagboard or butcher paper
Construction paper, white or light brown;
about 8 1/2" by 13".
Pens
Markers
Optional: Photocopies of ingredient cards from above activity
Glue sticks

preparation If you have time, photocopy the picture ingredient cards, making several copies of each one. Using the original picture ingredient cards, make one big picture recipe chart. Put it up near the table where the children will be making their recipe books. To make blank recipe books, take two pieces of paper and fold them over to make a notebook. Staple along the fold. After stapling, cut around the notebook to make an egg shape. If you have time, make your own book and entitle it "My Omelet Recipe Book by (your name.)" Inside, draw pictures and write the words of each food item you used, as well as the amount of each ingredient. Write about what you did to make an omelet. On the children's work table, near the recipe chart, set out the blank recipe books, pens, markers, and (optional) picture card photocopies and glue sticks.

directions   As the children are eating their omelets, show them your omelet recipe book or the chart, and say: "I decided to write down exactly how I made my omelet, so that if I want to make it again, I'll know how." Go through the chart or your book, and encourage the children to interpret as many of the picture signs as possible. Ask the kids if they'd like to make their own recipe books. There are a variety of options. They can glue the photocopied pictures in their books, copy down words from the picture chart, make up their own words and letters and write them, have you take story dictation, or ask you to write down other words for them to copy. Some children use a combination of these techniques. Speaking and listening skills will be developed as the children work together at the writing center, and/or during the next day's introductory activities when you invite children to show and tell about their recipe books. Most likely there'll be a wide variety in the vegetables the children chose for their omelets. This is fun to comment on and compare.

LANGUAGE/DRAMATIC PLAY:
The Egg Puppet Story

objective   Develop speaking, listening and reading skills; stimulate imagination and creative use of language.

materials   Brown and white construction paper
Popsicle sticks or tongue depressors
Tagboard or foam core

Poem: Six little eggs sitting in a carton,
one rolled away and stayed in the garden.
That left five but one fell out;
that left four without a doubt.
They heard a crack, one more was gone.
That leaves three to finish this song.
One wanted to leave, but what a gamble —
She took the jump and she got scrambled.
That left two, but I beg your pardon —
one eggshell bottom stuck to the carton.
That left one, but her shell did break —
She ended up in a chocolate cake!

preparation Use construction paper to make six egg shapes to stick on the tagboard or foam core. Make half the eggs brown ones, and make sure they all have different faces. Glue the tagboard or foam core puppets to the popsicle sticks and let them dry. Decide what will make the best puppet theater for you — a table turned over on its side, a large box with a square hole cut out; or a blanket draped across a broom pole. Set up the one that is best for you.

directions During introductory activities, use the puppets to tell the children the rhyme. Tape double-sided tape onto the edge of a table, so that you can stick on the puppets you don't have hands to hold. After telling the children the poem, show them your puppet theater, and ask them what they could do with it. Most likely, someone will suggest using the egg puppets. Say the poem many times during introductory activities to help the children learn it. You can vary the way you say it: adapt it as a fingerplay, use plastic eggs in an egg carton, or make felt eggs for a flannel board.

SCIENCE:
Egg Float

objective Facilitate scientific observation of what an egg does in fresh water compared to what an egg does in salty water; develop fine motor skills; develop all components of language: speaking, listening, writing, reading.

materials
Large piece of butcher paper
A fresh egg for each child
A large container of salt
A clear plastic container for each child
Popsicle sticks
Spoons
Water in pitchers
Writing sheets saying: "How many spoonfuls of salt does it take to make an egg float?"
Markers
Pens

Flat rectangular trays, like cafeteria trays
Picture sign saying: "Pour water in your cup. Put an egg in.
Add spoonfuls of salt. What happens?"
A round work table

preparation   Eggs that are old have more air in them that fresh eggs, and will even float in unsalted water. This could constitute another science experiment, but for this project, in order to see what eggs do in salt water, make sure your eggs are fresh. You may want to use tubs or a sensory table for this activity. If you use tubs, the trays work well to delineate individual space. Arrange an egg, clear container, popsicle stick, water, and a pitcher of water on each tray. You can pour a substantial amount of salt into two bowls, add several spoons, and put one near each end of the table. Put the picture sign in a prominent place nearby, as well as the butcher paper, which will be a prediction chart.

directions   As the children follow the directions of the activity sign by pouring water and adding and stirring salt, ask them what they think will happen to their eggs as they stir in the salt. Using an alternate color of marker for each answer, write down their responses. Also, let the kids know that if they want to keep count of how many spoonfuls of salt they put in, they can write the number down on their egg float experiment writing sheets. Ask the kids what they notice as the eggs begin to rise. (They may have to stir for a good five minutes, and they shouldn't scrimp on the salt.) Read their predictions back to them near the end of the activity, and ask if anyone wants to show and talk about their writing sheets to the rest of the group. Another fun way to stimulate language is to use your puppet to ask the kids about the experiment. Have your puppet ask questions about what the kids are doing and noticing.

LANGUAGE:
Egg Badge

objective   Stimulate vocabulary; develop speaking skills.

materials   Paper, brown and white
Double-sided tape

preparation   Cut out enough egg-shaped badges so that there is one for each child. Write on some: "Ask me about my egg experiment!", and leave some blank for kids who want to write their own words. Tear off double-sided tape strips. Affix a badge to yourself.

directions   When the children notice your badge, tell them what it says, and ask them if they would like one of their own.

EXTENDING THE CONCEPT

art   For the dramatic play activity, you may want to have the children make their own egg puppets. Provide plenty of pre-cut brown and white egg shapes for younger children to decorate or draw egg outlines for them to cut themselves. Provide glue and popsicle sticks so that the kids can make handles for their puppets.

gross motor   For the nature box egg carton art activity, you may want to have a nature walk so that the children can hunt for their own treasures. Provide them with baggies or paper bags in which to collect their discoveries, and after the egg carton nature boxes are decorated, they can transfer all their treasures.

sensory: After the math activity with the plastic eggshells, put objects in the shells that will vary in sound and/or weight when shaken (rice, a pebble, a heavy bolt, etc.) and play a game with the kids. Have them feel or shake the egg, and guess what's inside.

science   As mentioned above, old eggs will float in plain water. Do a comparison between what old and fresh eggs do in water, and then break them open to see if you can spot differences inside. (Your eggs shouldn't be <u>too</u> old. Eggs that are several weeks old are usually not rotten.)

science   After reading *Green Eggs And Ham*, make scrambled eggs and add a very small drop of blue food coloring to each yellow scrambled egg. What happens?

LITERATURE

*Turner, Dorothy, *Eggs*, CarolRhoda Books, 1989 (Raises the issue of factory farming. Terrific photographs, but quite a lot of text. You may want to talk the children through it, or read selectively.)

*Troughton, Joanna, *The Quail's Egg*, Bedrick/Blackie, 1988 (A tale from Sri Lanka)

Seuss, Dr., *Green Eggs And Ham*, Random House, 1960

Teaching From

WORK RELATED OBJECTS

Gizmos

Paper

Paperclips

Press and slide
and click and snap;
important things
go clunket-clack.

THEME: gizmos

machines, mechanisms, metal objects

For convenience, the word "gizmo" is used to embrace small machines, mechanisms, as well as metal objects that interact with, or are part of, mechanisms. The word "mechanism" will probably take the children some time to learn, so you'll probably want to reinforce this word frequently, and allow some time to pass before you introduce the word gizmo. Basically, gizmo (it is in the dictionary!) is slang for mechanism. With older kids, you may be able to introduce both words on the same day without causing confusion. Even simple household items like click-top pens and staplers provide mechanical lessons. If you can gather some defunct machines for this unit, so much the better. The first important step in this unit is to assess your gizmos from a safety perspective. Remove all parts that are sharp, rusty, or made of easily broken glass.

INTRODUCTORY ACTIVITIES

ATTENTION GRABBER

Take a nut and bolt from the math activity below, and put them in a tin with a top on it. It will feel heavy, and will also make quite a sound when shaken. When the kids have gathered, pass around the tin. Let them feel it and shake it. When everyone has had a chance to hold the tin and guess its contents, open the tin together and examine the nut and bolt.

INTRODUCTORY DISCUSSION

objective   Introduce the theme; develop speaking skills; expand vocabulary.

materials   Gizmo rhyme
Magazines with pictures of people using machines (National Geographic is a surprisingly good source)

directions   Read the poem to the children at least twice. Tell the kids that a thing that does a job for us, and has moving parts is called a machine. With younger children, while you say it you can tap the word on your knees, noses, ankles, and so forth. Together, look at all the pictures you found in the magazines and name the objects. Ask: "What is the machine or object that person has? What is that person doing?" Ask the children if they have any of the objects or machines that are in the pictures, at their own houses. Do they have any machines at home that aren't in the pictures? Ask them to talk about how the machines at their houses work. As the children talk about the machines at home, distinguish between big machines and little ones.

MUSIC/MOVEMENT: Clock Song

objective   Develop sense of rhythm; develop cognition through memorization of words and music; help children enjoy singing.

materials   To the tune of I'm A Little Teapot:
I'm a little clock that will not stop,
hear me go tick tock tick tock.
My doors pop open when it's noon,
    and you will hear "cuckoo cuckoo."

directions For "I'm a little clock that will not stop," move your arms around like the hands of a clock. For "hear me go tick tock tick tock," wag your pointer finger back and forth in time to the song. For "My doors pop open when it's noon," put your hands side by side and then swing them open. For "and you will hear 'cuckoo cuckoo,'" cup your hands around your mouth.

SOCIAL STUDIES:
Who Uses Machines?

objective Introduce the concept that anyone can use machines.

materials Photographs of people from diverse cultures and lifestyles using small machines (from magazines).
Drawings at right
Tagboard
Glue

preparation Glue the pictures onto the tagboard. The pictures at right are provided in case you're unable to find people of diverse cultures using machines in magazine pictures — something which can be difficult. You can color in the illustrations provided to make them more attractive.

directions Ask the children about the machines in their homes. Who uses the machines? Look at the pictures on the poster together. The discussion may lead to what the children see on television. This is a good opportunity to talk about what's real and what's not, and how much of what's on television is different from what real people are like and what real people do.

ACTIVITY CENTERS

ART:
Gizmo Creation

objective Develop creative ability and expression; develop fine motor skills; develop writing skills and familiarity with written numbers.

materials

Styrofoam packing part blocks
Markers
Flat top tacks
Plastic milk caps
Paper fasteners
Dials
Tagboard
Small jingle bells (available at craft shops)
Stapler
Spools
Round, thin sticks (available at craft shops)
Magnet squares (available at craft shops)
Yarn
Small jewelry
Plastic lids
Paperclips
Skewer
Exacto knife of razor blade

preparation Collect and prepare as many of the above as you have time for. The above list, and the following preparation instructions are intended only to give you ideas. Your kids will still have fun with this project even if you can only provide half the suggested materials. The styrofoam blocks are intended as the machines, and there are a number of contrivances that can be attached to them: dials and arrows that spin, flaps that open, knobs that turn, spools that slide, and compartments with covers that fasten. Also, the amount of preparation you put in on these attachments should depend on the age of your children: older children will probably prefer to make their own; younger children will need some pre-made parts. To make a knob or dial, punch a hole in the middle of a milk cap with a skewer. Push a paper fastener through the hole and then push the prongs into the styrofoam block. The outside of the milk cap should be on the outside of the styrofoam for a knob; for a dial, the inside of the milk cap should be on the outside of the styrofoam. Pointer dials can be made by cutting a pointer dial shape out of a plastic lid, and by using a paper fastener, attaching the dial to styrofoam in the same way as the milk caps. Styrofoam is hard to write on, so cut out dial and knob platforms from tagboard. These are just tagboard circles, the diameter of which should depend on the size of your styrofoam blocks. Write numbers, letters or symbols on some of your dial platforms, and leave others blank. You or the kids can put the platforms under the dials, and simultaneously push paper fasteners through the end of the dial and the center of the dial platform. Before pushing the prongs into the styrofoam, put some glue on the back of the dial platform, but not near the center, so that the dial platform is more securely attached. Using an exacto knife, carve niches and cavities in the

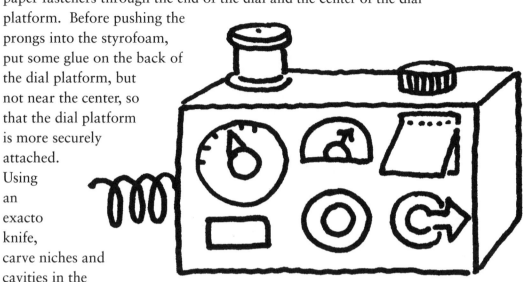

styrofoam blocks, and also cut out tagboard flaps. The size and shape of the flaps will depend on the size and shape of the cavities. Make a fold at the end of each flap that is about a half inch from one edge. This half-inch fold will be attached to the styrofoam; the rest of the flap will be lifted up and down. To attach the flap, dip tacks into glue, and punch them through the half inch base of the flap and into the styrofoam. To make the flap fasten, glue a magnet square onto the styrofoam at the top of the cavity, and a paperclip onto the end of the inside of the flap. To make sliding spools, you can stick round, thin sticks straight into your styrofoam base, and if you like, glue a styrofoam block on the top, so that the spool won't come off. Or, you may want the spool to be removable. Spread all materials out on the work surface. Make a machine yourself. Write numbers, letters, and/or symbols around your dials and knobs. Decide what kind it's going to be — the one I made was a sticker machine. When I turned the dial, spun the spool, slid the other spools, opened a small flap and turned the knob inside, and then jingled the bells, there was a sticker waiting when I opened the big compartment.

directions During introductory activities, show the children your machine. Let them operate whatever dials, knobs, flaps, and so forth that you put on your machine. Show the kids all the materials on the work table, and then ask what they could do with them. Go with the suggestions you get. Have a show and tell of machines during one day's introductory activities. Because of the time involved in the actual construction of machines and their decoration, this can be an on-going activity throughout the unit.

ART:
Metal Creation

objective   Develop fine motor skills; facilitate creative expression.

materials   Tagboard squares
Small screws
Small nuts
Small washers
Paper fasteners
Key rings
Any small, safe metal objects available at hardware stores
Glue
Glue brushes

preparation   Spread all materials out on the table so that the children have access to all materials.

directions   Invite the kids to explore and use the materials.

MATH:
Nuts And Bolts Match

objective   Facilitate matching exercise; develop mechanical competence; facilitate rational counting and subtracting; develop fine motor skills through screwing and unscrewing nuts and bolts.

materials   Matching nuts and bolts varying in size and diameter from very large and heavy, to small (available at hardware stores very inexpensively)
Writing sheets
Three containers that are very different in shape
Pens

preparation   Unscrew all the nuts from the bolts and set them out on a tray. I don't find a sign necessary for this activity — children seem to know instinctively to match and screw them. Real metal nuts and bolts from a

hardware store are far more satisfactory than toy plastic ones. For older children, divide matched nuts and bolts between the three containers and put writing sheets and pens next to them. To make your writing sheets, you'll have to draw your container symbols according to the shapes of your own containers, and write next to each symbol, "How many nuts (or bolts) in this container?"

directions Encourage the children to explore the materials.

MATH/SENSORY:
How Heavy?

objective Provide experience in comparing weights; facilitate experience in balancing weights; provide sensory experience with parts of gizmos.

materials
- Nuts and bolts, including large, heavy ones
- Keys
- Key rings
- Paper fasteners
- Washers
- Coins
- Balancing scales
- Sensory table, if possible
- Scoops

preparation Put all materials in the sensory table. If you don't have a sensory table, put the balancing scales in the largest tub you have.

directions Invite the children to explore the materials.

LANGUAGE/DRAMATIC PLAY:
Ms. Gizmo Flannel Board Story

objective Stimulate creative use of language; develop speaking and listening skills.

materials
- Flannel Board Story below
- Flannel board pieces on page 233
- large square of felt for "machine"
- "Two People May Be Here" sign

preparation   During the day's introductory activities, tell the children the flannel board story and let them know that the flannel pieces and the flannel board will be available for them to use during the morning's activities. A primary goal of this flannel board story is to expand the children's vocabulary, so when you tell it, point to each object as it is mentioned and encourage the kids to say the names with you. Before you begin, discuss the word "install" with the kids. Also, discuss with the children the difference between a button that you push on a machine, and a button on a sweater or shirt. Ask the kids if they have machines with buttons at home. Glue pictures of toys and candy onto felt. Put them under the flap to be discovered at the end of the story when Ms. Gizmo lifts up the door of the machine.

directions   Enjoy the stories you overhear!

story   Once upon a time there was an inventor by the name of Ms. Gizmo. [Put Ms. Gizmo character on the flannel board.] What did she invent? All sorts of wonderful things. A machine that would clean up a messy bedroom at the touch of a button. A toy robot that would walk and talk. And a gum ball machine that never ran out of gumballs. But she was tired of all these things now, and decided that this time, she'd invent the most magical, most wonderful machine that had ever been invented in the world. Ms. Gizmo had to build many things onto such a wonderful machine, as you can well imagine. [Put large felt square on board as machine base]. There had to be a way to turn the machine on, so Ms. Gizmo had to install a lock in the machine, and there was a key to go with it. [Put lock on machine, and the key nearby.] Now the machine had a lock and a key. Ms. Gizmo had to install a lever, [Put the lever on the machine.] so now the machine had a lock, a key, and a lever. She had to screw on a round part with many numbers on it so that she could set a dial at the right number. [Place the dial on the machine.] So now the machine had a lock, a key, a lever and a dial. The machine had to have a button on it, so Ms. Gizmo built a button. [Place the button on the machine.] So now the machine had a lock, a key, a lever, a dial, and a button. There had to be a switch on the machine, so she installed a switch. [Place switch on machine.] So now the machine had a lock, a key, a lever, a dial, a button and a switch. There had to be a keyboard to type words into the machines computer of the machine, so Ms. Gizmo installed a keyboard. [Place keyboard on machine.] So now the machine had a lock, a key, a lever, a dial, a button, a switch, and a keyboard. There had to be a monitor on the machine, so that Ms. Gizmo could see what she typed, so she built a monitor into the machine. [Put monitor on machine.] So now the machine had a lock, a key, a lever, a dial, a button, a switch, a keyboard, and a monitor. And finally, Ms. Gizmo put a steering wheel on the most magical, wonderful machine. [Put the steering wheel on the machine.] So now the machine had a lock, a key, a lever, a dial, a button, a switch, a keyboard, a monitor and a steering wheel. Finally the moment came to try the most magical, wonderful machine and see if it

worked. Ms. Gizmo turned the key in the lock, pulled down the lever, spun the dial, pushed the button, flipped the switch, punched in orders on the keyboard, read the monitor, and turned the steering wheel. The most magical, wonderful machine made some very odd noises. It clunked and clacked and whirred and shuddered. Ms. Gizmo wondered and wondered if it would work. All of a sudden there was a loud bang, and the machine was silent. Ms. Gizmo lifted up the door of the machine, and guess what she found? [Hold up each flannel piece under the flap, and have the children name the object on it.] Guess what kind of a magical, wonderful machine Ms. Gizmo had invented? A machine that would give her whatever she wished for!
THE END.

SCIENCE:
How Do Gizmo Parts Work?

objective Develop mechanical competence; help children understand how moving mechanical parts work; develop observation skills; encourage individual exploration.

materials Nuts and bolts
A jar and screw lid (preferably plastic)
A clamp
Spray mechanism from a spray bottle
If possible, toy pipes and joints that screw onto each other
A "One Person May Be Here" sign
A plastic magnifying glass
Two click pens; one dismantled
Available at hardware stores: Snap bolts
Eye pulleys
Locks and keys
Hinges
Springs
Rollers

preparation Set all materials out on a table.

directions   Encourage exploration of all materials. Talk to the kids about what they observe: how the parts move, how the parts interact, how the gadgets work.

GROSS MOTOR:
Gizmo Fishing

objective   Develop hand/eye coordination; develop large arm muscles.

materials   Small metal objects: washers, coins, keys, and so forth
Small horseshoe magnets
Sticks (craft stores or nature)
String
Hole punch

preparation   Tie string around the middle of each magnet and attach the other end of each string length to a stick, to make magnetic fishing rods. The string lengths should depend on the heights of your kids. Arrange your gizmos on the floor. (Be sure to save your magnetic fishing rods for the Whingy Whiner unit.)

directions   Invite the kids to fish for gizmos. Point out the magnets on the ends of the rods. Discuss which gizmos can be picked up by the magnets and which ones can't — how are they different?

EXTENDING THE CONCEPT

science   If possible, try to obtain or borrow some gear toy sets: Cog Labyrinth by Brio, Rotello by Quercetti, or Wonderwheels by Little Hands.

science   Give the children rotary beaters, warm water, and liquid soap. How do the beaters work? What happens when they mix the water and soap, and beat it with the rotary beaters? (If the beaters are too large, the handles may be difficult for young children to turn.)

crafts/art   Make necklaces by threading yarn through nuts and washers.

math   If you can gather a collection of old keys (friends, parents, and neighbors may be able to help), arrange several on the glass of a photocopier, and make a copy. Make a set of three or four copies in this way, using different keys for each one, and then cover the copies with contact paper on both sides. Put the keys and the copies out on trays for the children to match.

LITERATURE

*Ardley, Neil, *The Science Book Of Mechanics*, HBJ Gulliver Books, 1992
Horvatic, Anne, *Simple Machines*, E.P. Dutton, 1989 (Terrific pictures, but unfortunately, despite lots of people, no cultural diversity of any kind.)
Hoban, Tana, *Round And Round And Round*, Scholastic Inc. 1983
Berenstain, Stan and Jan, *Bears On Wheels*, Random House, 1969

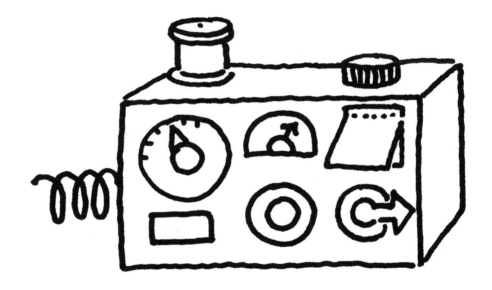

Wind makes paper

skitter-scutter,

lots of litter

in the gutter.

THEME: paper

There are so many differently colored and textured papers, that this unit lends itself naturally to sensory-oriented activities. Once again, you can begin collecting what you need weeks ahead of time. The vast majority of art activities involve paper, which means there are hundreds of activities that would fit right into this unit. The two mentioned here focus on the sensory experience of paper. The second art project lists embossed paper and business cards as materials. Duplicating shops or stationers may donate samples of these materials if you say why you need them.

INTRODUCTORY ACTIVITIES

ATTENTION GRABBER

When the children are gathered, ask them to close their eyes. Take a piece of paper, and using only one hand, bend and flap it. Ask the children if they can guess what is making the sound. When they see the paper in your hand, ask them to guess what you'll be talking about for the next few days.

INTRODUCTORY DISCUSSION

objective   Introduce the theme; develop speaking and listening skills; expand vocabulary; encourage expression of feelings and perceptions.

materials   Paper rhyme

directions   Read the rhyme to the children at least twice. Ask them what these words mean: litter, gutter, skitter, scutter. Explain or clarify these words if necessary. Ask them if they've ever seen garbage in a gutter.

MUSIC/MOVEMENT:
The Paper Song

objective   Develop cognition through memorization of words and related actions; develop enjoyment of singing and appreciation of music.

materials   To the tune of Twinkle, twinkle little star:
Wind makes paper skitter-scutter,
lots of litter in the gutter.
Catch that paper in a flash,
throw it, stuff it in the trash.
There they go a-skitter scutter,
fewer papers in the gutter.

Flap and flutter, windy day —
paper pieces sail away.
Catch that paper in a flash,
throw it, stuff it in the trash.
Flap and flutter, windy day,
that garbage did not get away.

directions   For "Wind makes paper skitter-scutter, lots of litter in the gutter," pretend to be a piece of paper being blown by the wind. Put your arms out, and pretend the wind is blowing you down a street. For "Catch that paper in a flash, throw it, stuff it in the trash," pretend to pick up paper from the ground and throw and stuff pieces into a garbage can. For "There they go a-skitter scutter," put your hand over your eyes as if you're looking down the street. For "fewer papers in the gutter," rub your hands in satisfaction. Repeat the actions for each line in the first verse for the second verse.

GROSS MOTOR/SOCIAL STUDIES:
Litter Pick Up

objective Exercise large muscle groups; help develop an awareness of the prevalence of littering and its impact; help develop a community conscience by picking up litter.

materials Magazine or book picture of a littered street
Medium sized paper or plastic bags

preparation Before you go out to pick up litter, show the children the picture of a littered street. Ask: "Do you think the street in this picture is a pretty one? Why? Where should we put paper garbage when we're finished with it — is it O.K. just to throw it down on the ground wherever we happen to be?" Let the children know that you're all going to go out to pick up any litter you see, but that you're only going to pick up <u>paper</u> litter. (You don't want the kids picking up glass or tin.) Ask them: "When we're on our walk, is it O.K. to pick up glass? What if you see a nail? Are we going to pick up anything that's not paper?"

directions Give each child a bag, and set out on your walk. Try to go to an area that does not have heavy traffic on the roads, otherwise, you may want to limit your litter search to paper garbage that's on the sidewalk.

ACTIVITY CENTERS

ART:
Paper Construction

objective Develop fine motor, including cutting, skills; develop decision-making abilities by providing lots of interesting materials to choose from; facilitate creative expression; introduce fact that flat paper can be made into dimensional objects; develop all components of language: reading, writing, speaking and listening.

materials Paper shapes on pages 17-18
Glue
Construction paper pages
Glue brushes
Scissors

preparation Have all materials available on the work table. Make a paper construction yourself, and write words on your page about what you made and/or how you made it.

directions During the introductory activities, show the children your paper construction, and read them the words you wrote. Show them the materials on the activity table, and encourage the kids to explore the materials. Older children will want to make their own paper shapes, and you can help them with this. When the kids are finished making their paper constructions, ask them if they would like any words to be written about them. Either take dictation, or write down their words for them to copy onto their paper constructions themselves. Near the end of the activities, gather together again and invite children to show, and tell about, their creations.

ART/LANGUAGE:
Paper Texture Collage

objective Enable children to explore different paper textures; develop creative expression; develop fine motor skills.

materials
Construction paper
Sand paper
Wax paper
Crepe paper
Tissue paper
Embossed paper
Brown bag paper
Newspaper
Facial tissue paper
Any other interestingly textured paper you find
Glue
Glue brushes
Stapler

preparation Cut out construction paper into 12" by 9" sheets. Taking two pieces, fold them over to make a 6" by 9" book, and staple twice along the 9" fold. Make one book for each child, then create your own paper texture book. Choose from the differently textured papers listed above, and glue one on each page. Write a few words about each — what you like about the piece of paper, the color it is, what it feels like. Arrange all materials on the work table. Save samples of all the above papers for the Paper Count activity below.

directions   During the introductory activities, read the children your paper texture book. Invite them to come and feel each texture. (Print on business cards can be felt.) Let the children know that if they would like to make their own texture books, the materials are available on the art table. When the children finish gluing their paper pieces, ask them if they would like words written about the papers they chose. Take dictation or write down the children's words for them to copy into their books. When each book is completed, read it back to the child, and/or encourage her/him to tell or 'read' it to you.

LANGUAGE/DRAMATIC PLAY/ART:
Paper Puppets

objective   Enable children to act out real life situations; develop all components of language: reading, writing, speaking and listening.

materials
Tagboard, white
Tagboard, brown or
Brown construction paper
Markers
Crayons
Popsicle sticks or tongue depressors
Yarn: red, yellow, brown, black
Glue
Glue brushes
Fabric scraps
Wallpaper samples
Double-sided tape
Tagboard scrap
Optional: Any other collage materials

preparation   If you aren't able to find brown tagboard, take a sheet of white, and on it put long strips, horizontally and vertically, of double-sided tape. Press the brown pieces of construction paper on. Cut out puppet shapes from the white and brown tagboard and, if you work with younger children, glue each one to a stick yourself. Older children can carry this step out for themselves. Cut yellow, red, brown and black yarn into strands that will be long enough or short enough to provide hair for the puppets. Cut out clothes shapes from fabric scraps or wallpaper samples. Stores are often willing to donate old sample books. Set out all materials on work surface. Make one puppet for yourself, by coloring the puppet and/or using yarn and fabric scraps for clothes and hair. Decide on a name for your puppet and write it on the back.

directions   During introductory activities, show the children the tagboard scrap and tell them its name. Let them examine the tagboard to see the layers of paper that made it. Tell the kids that you made something from tagboard and paper.

Give your puppet a personality and use it to interact with the children. After a few minutes, turn the puppet around, and show the children the puppet's name on its back. Spell out the letters and read the name. Let the kids know that if they want to make their own puppets, the materials are available on a table. Children may want to make animals instead of people, and they can use the additional (optional) collage materials for this. After the children have decorated the tagboard cutouts, ask them if they have names for their puppets, and if they want the names written on the back. Take dictation or help the kids write their own letters. When the puppets are dry, provide a puppet theater in which the children can use them.

MATH/SENSORY:
Texture Envelopes

objective   Facilitate rational counting; provide a sensory experience; develop all components of language: reading, writing, speaking and listening; facilitate texture matching.

materials
Butcher paper
Sandpaper
Wax paper
Paper towel
Brown paper bag
Newspaper
Embossed paper if possible
Other textured papers
Envelopes
Glue or glue stick
Pens
Two trays
For chart: 1" by 1" samples of above papers
Two-person work table
A "Two people may be here" sign

preparation   In this activity, you're going to make two sets of envelopes, each envelope containing a number of pieces of a particular texture of paper to be counted by the children. To prepare the envelopes, glue a sample on the outside of the kind of paper you're going to put inside. Vary the number of samples you put in each one, but keep in mind how high your children can count. For example, you might have four pieces of wax paper in the wax paper envelope, seven pieces of sandpaper in the sandpaper envelope, and so forth. Also, save 1" by 1" samples of the different textures for your chart. For the chart, make one column of the 1" by 1" paper samples, and as a header to this column, write: "How many pieces of this paper in your envelope?" Make additional columns for each of the children's responses, and heading each column with a student's name. Put each set of paper counting envelopes on a tray. Arrange each set of materials so that two children will be working face to face, and set the "Two people may be here" sign above the table.

directions   Encourage the children to explore the materials. Take your tagboard puppet that you made in the Art activity above, and using its personality, ask the children what they're doing. Have children take turns marking their responses on the chart.

SCIENCE:
Absorbing Experiment

objective   Facilitate an understanding of what kinds of materials absorb water and what kinds of paper repel water; facilitate all components of language: reading, writing, speaking and listening.

materials
Wax paper
Paper towels
Cardboard
White or off-white construction paper
Eye or medicine droppers
Containers of water
Writing sheets (described below)
Pens
A puppet of your choosing
Plastic or styrofoam trays
Picture sign saying: "What do wax paper, paper towel, and cardboard do when you drop water on them?"
Tin foil
Fabric

preparation   Set one sample of each kind of paper on each tray, accompanied by one eye dropper and one container of water. To make the writing sheets, make three columns on a page. In the first column, list the materials the children will be testing for absorbency. In the second, write "absorbs water" next to each kind of paper with a smiley face and a line for them to mark; and in the third column, write, "doesn't absorb water" for each paper type with a frowny face and a line. Set writing sheets and pens near to the trays but not on them, and hang the picture sign in a visible place near the work table.

directions   During the introductory activities, take a water dropper filled with water, the tin foil, and a piece of fabric. Drop a few water drops on the fabric, and when the kids see it sink in, tell them that the word for that is "absorb." The fabric absorbs the water. With younger kids you may want to tap the word on your knees, noses, ankles and so forth while saying the word several times. Next, drop a few drops of water on the tin foil. Ask the kids what the water is doing. When they see it sitting on top of the foil, tell them that the foil is "repelling" the water. That means it won't let the water sink in. Repeat the above tapping/repeating exercise for the word repel with younger children. Tell the kids that you wonder if there are certain papers that absorb or repel water, and let them know that if they want to do a science experiment with paper and water, that different kinds of paper are available on the table. Show them the writing sheets, and help them interpret and read the symbols and words on them. Let the kids know that the writing sheets are for anyone who wants to record her/his science experiment results. After the kids have had a chance to use the materials, use your puppet to ask the children what they're doing.

EXTENDING THE CONCEPT

music Using rhythm sticks or popsicle sticks, chant the rhyme in the music and movement activity, and tap your sticks together to keep rhythm.

science What papers float? Give the children a variety of differently textured paper to see which ones float. Talk about the connection between absorbing water and sinking quickly.

art Dip paper in trays of water, and then give the children chalk or old markers to draw with on the paper. If you use markers, be prepared to throw the markers out after the activity.

LITERATURE

Curtis, Neil, & Greenland, Peter, *I Wonder How Paper Is Made*, Lerner Publications, 1992
*Cosner, Sharon, *Paper Through The Ages*, CarolRhoda Books, 1984
Lohf, Sabrina, *Things I Can Make With Paper*, Chronicle Books, 1989 (Wonderful photographs)
*Bang, Molly, *The Paper Crane*, Greenwillow Books, 1985

Paperclips

a-clangle clingle,

clinking, chinking,

jangle, jingle.

THEME: paperclips

Paperclips are inexpensive and they come in many types and sizes. Again, if you need help gathering a large and diverse collection, ask your friends, relatives and parents to help you collect them. Stores may be willing to donate a few packages or boxes or paperclips if you let proprietors know what they're for. The variety of paperclips include: differently colored vinyl covered clips, differently colored plastic clips, glittery clips, metal clips, jumbo sized clips, butterfly clips, and squeeze clips of different sizes.

INTRODUCTORY ACTIVITIES

ATTENTION GRABBER

Put some paperclips in a tin box and shake it. Pass it around to the children so that everyone has a chance to shake it. Ask the kids to guess what's inside. After everyone's made a guess, open the tin and pass it around to the children. What are they and what are they for? Have some paper handy to slide some paperclips over.

INTRODUCTORY DISCUSSION

objective Introduce the theme; stimulate discussion and expression of ideas; develop cognition and observation skills; familiarize children with rational counting and written numbers.

materials   A children's book with an office setting; Mommy's Office by Barbara Shook Hazen is a good one for this purpose
Assortment of paperclip types
Butcher paper chart
Clear tape
Marker

directions Look through the pictures in the book Mommy's Office or another children's book with an office setting. Point to a desk in a picture, and ask children what kinds of things they think they might find in an office desk drawer. If no one else does, mention paperclips. Read the paperclip rhyme at least twice. Show the children your paperclip collection and ask them to guess what you'll be working with and talking about for the next few days.

MUSIC/MOVEMENT/SENSORY:
Paperclip Song

objective Develop cognition by memorizing words and related actions; help children enjoy singing; develop muscle control; develop listening skills.

materials   Yogurt cups
Paperclips

To the tune of Twinkle twinkle little star:
Paperclips a-jingle jangle,
Shake them, hear them clingle clangle.
Shake them softly, shake them hard,
Slide them around, but not too hard,
Paperclips a-jingle jangle,
Shake them, hear them clingle clangle.

preparation Provide each child with some regular, metal paperclips in a plastic yogurt container.

directions Follow the directions of the song. For "Slide them around, but not too hard," slowly tip your yogurt cup to make the clips slide slowly across the container bottom. After singing the song a few times, tell the children that you're going to open your ears to the different sounds that are made with the different actions. Listening carefully, shake the clips softly, then shake them hard, and then tip your cups and make the clips slide. Ask the children if the sounds are different.

ACTIVITY CENTERS

ART:
Paperclip Structures

objective   Provide art experience with unusual materials; develop fine motor skills; facilitate creative expression.

materials
- Paperclips of all kinds, including vinyl covered ones
- Tagboard cut to page size
- Glue
- Dry tempera
- Glue brushes
- Double-sided tape

preparation   Add dry tempera to the glue to color it. Put all materials out on the activity table. Tear off many small strips of double-sided tape, and stick them on the edge of the table. Make a paperclip structure yourself by gluing or sticking paperclips on top of paperclips. The double-sided tape helps when you're building height. Let your paperclip structure dry.

directions   During the day's introductory activities, show the kids your paperclip structure. Let them touch it gently, and show them the materials on the activity table, in case they'd like to build their own.

ART:
Paperclip Necklaces And Bracelets

objective   Develop fine motor skills; develop self-esteem by providing children with the opportunity to make their own jewelry to keep; develop cognition by identifying different colors combined with math activity below.

materials
- Differently colored vinyl paperclips
- String
- Masking tape
- Small pieces of paper
- Hole punch
- Twist ties

preparation   Older children will be able to make straight paperclip chains, but younger children will need to thread the clips onto string. For this purpose, cut off lengths of string and roll a small strip of masking tape around one end to make the end stiff, and easier to thread. Punch one hole in each piece of paper. Small children can thread the paper onto their string. Older children can use twist ties to attach the paper to their paperclip chain. Set all materials out on a table. Make a paper chain necklace or bracelet yourself and put it on. I usually thread the string through each paperclip twice.

directions During introductory activities, show the children your bracelet or necklace. Let them know that if they would like to make one themselves, the materials are available on a work table. As the children make their chains, discuss the names of the colors with them in a casual way. The paper tags are for names, as well as the math activity below.

MATH/LANGUAGE:
Paperclip Count

objective Facilitate rational counting; develop all components of language: reading, writing, speaking and listening skills.

materials Bracelets and necklaces made in above activity
Pens
Puppet (optional)

preparation As the children work on their chains, take yours off. Casually say: "I know what I'm going to do — I'm going to count how many paperclips are on my chain, and I'm going to write that number on my tag." Count your paperclips and write the number on your tag. Show your written number to any children who are interested. Then say: "My favorite colored clip on my bracelet is the X one. I think I'll write that down, too." When the kids have complete their chains, ask them if they want to count the number of clips on it. Take dictation from them in regard to anything else they want to say about their bracelets/necklaces. Some kids may want you to write down their words first so that they can copy them onto the tags. Some time during the day, gather together again, and encourage each child to show and tell her/his bracelet/necklace or use a puppet's personality to ask the kids about what they made.

MATH:
Paperclip Match

objective Facilitate rational counting; provide matching experience; provide classification activity for older children; develop sense of autonomy by providing a one-person work station.

materials
Small boxes or containers — 7 or 8
A wide variety of differently shaped, sized, and colored paperclips.
Glue or glue stick
Paper
Pen
A "One Person May Be Here" sign
Picture sign saying: "How many paperclips in each container?"
Small, one-person work table

preparation In this activity, you're going to put a number of one kind of paperclip in each box to be counted by the children. To prepare the boxes or containers, glue on the outside of the box one sample of the kind of clip you're putting inside. Decide how many should go inside by how high your children are counting. For younger children, put only one color and one size in each box or container. For older children though, you may want to make the activity more challenging. For example, divide the paperclips by kind — vinyl colored clips of different colors in one box, metal clips of different sizes in another, plastic clips of different colors in another, and so forth. Set all materials out on the table, and place the signs prominently. The paper and pen is for older children who like to write down how many objects they counted.

directions Encourage the children to explore the materials.

SCIENCE:
Magnets And Paperclips

objective Facilitate scientific observation of the effect of magnets on paperclips; help children understand which materials are attracted to magnets and which aren't; develop all components of language arts: speaking, listening, reading and writing skills.

materials
Magnets
A wide variety of different clips, including vinyl covered and plastic clips.
Writing sheets that show the kinds of clip you have and ask: "Does the magnet pick up this kind of paperclip?"
Pens
Double-sided tape
Two-person work table.

preparation
Arrange all materials at the two-person work table so that two children will be working face to face. Make photocopies of the writing sheets, and using double-sided tape, stick on a sample of each clip to be tested by the magnet.

directions
If only one child is sitting at the table at a time, sit down on the opposite side, test the clips with your magnet, and talk to the child opposite you about what s/he is discovering, as well as what you're doing.

GROSS MOTOR/SOCIAL STUDIES:
Paperclip Trail

objective
Develop large muscles; develop observation skills; facilitate cooperative cleaning effort; emphasize the concept that when everyone helps with a chore, it makes less work for each individual; emphasize the concept of responsibility for materials used; emphasize the concept of fair distribution.

materials
Paperclips — vinyl covered clips of different colors are best
Stickers
Double-sided tape
Masking tape
Picture sign saying: "Follow the paperclip trail to a treasure!"

preparation
Decide on a spot where you are going to hide a treasure trove of stickers, one for each child. Lay a paperclip trail around the school or room that twists and turns, and eventually leads to the treasure trove. In places where the clips are likely to be kicked or scuffed, secure them with double-sided tape. If possible, arrange the clips so that children have to climb or crawl. On stairs, ladders, or under tables or tunnels, use double-sided tape to secure the clips, and put them along one side, rather than in the middle of the passage way. Also, the clips on your trail will be more inclined to stay put if you place them along baseboards and the sides of furniture, rather than in areas that are most heavily walked

over. The paperclips won't be immediately visible, but this is part of the game — children really have to use their eyes to spot the trail. Put a masking tape line on the ground where the trail begins, and put the sign beside it. (You could tape it to the back of a chair.)

directions During introductory activities, show the children the beginning of the paperclip trail. Tell them that at the end of the trail, there is something special for everyone, but that there is only one for each person. Ask the kids what will happen if one person takes more than one of the special somethings. After you've discussed this, ask the children what you should all do with the clips when the hunt is over. Should they be left where they are? If it isn't suggested that the clips should be picked up, mention this yourself. Ask the children who they think could pick the clips up. Talk about how much work it would be for one or two people, and how long it would take them. The children may suggest that everyone help, or you may end up throwing this suggestion out yourself. Another way to approach this, is by gathering everyone together <u>after</u> the day's activities, and having the clean up discussion then. If you know how many paperclips you used to make the trail, you could have a set number of clips for each child to pick up. Also, throughout the play period, you'll periodically have to rearrange the clips on the trail that are not stuck down, as well as go back after clean up time to pick off the tape. It's worth it though — kids love following the trail. When all the clips are picked up, talk about how fast they were cleaned up. Tell the kids how glad you are that everyone helped, and talk about what a lot of work it would have been for one person.

DRAMATIC PLAY:
Office

objective Allow children to assume varied roles; facilitate acting out of real-life situations; develop vocabulary and creativity; develop all components of language: reading, writing, speaking and listening skills.

materials As many of these as you can gather:
Old machines: typewriter, calculator, computer keyboard
Telephone
Staplers
Hole punches
Paperclips
Envelopes
Notepads
Receipt books
Pens
Telephone books
Old reports or printouts
Letterhead stationery
Business cards

preparation Set out all materials to simulate an office. If you do have a computer keyboard, you can make a monitor by using a box. You may be able to obtain computer brochures with photographs of monitors with actual documents, and you could glue one of these onto your box to simulate an active monitor.

directions Encourage the kids to explore the office, and when appropriate, be an office worker yourself.

EXTENDING THE CONCEPT

field trip If you can, organize a field trip to a friend's or parent's office. Take a tour that includes an explanation of the use of the machines in the office. If it has a photocopier, let the children make photocopies of their hands as souvenirs of the visit. Ask where the paperclips are kept, and see what kinds there are.

math Using differently colored vinyl covered paperclips, start patterns with them by gluing the clips onto tagboard, or by putting down a strip of double-sided tape and sticking the clips on. Double-sided tape has the added advantage of letting the children make new patterns on the same piece of tagboard.

art/ social studies Make a giant paperclip chain as a group. Stretch it out and see how much of the room it measures, and/or how many children can lie down next to it, toe to head.

language Make a language chart of where everybody's parents work. Make a graph of the results, and count how many parents work at home, how many in an office, and how many work in another type of work place.

LITERATURE

*Shook Hazen, Barbara, *Mommy's Office*, Athenaeum, 1992 (One page shows the central character making a paperclip chain.)
*Leiner, Katherine, *Both My Parents Work*, Franklin Watts, 1986 (When you read this, it's fun to ask the kids which workers in the book might work in offices.)
Schwartz, Amy, *Bea And Mr. Jones*, Bradbury Press, 1982

Teaching From
FANTASY

Ye Olde Spooky House

The Whingy Whiner

The boards of the
floors do creak and groan;
The wind outside does
howl and moan;
Sticky cobwebs hang
a-hither;
and shifting shadows
make you shiver.

ye old spooky house

This theme is a lot of fun, and of course, is perfect for Halloween. When making your own spooky house, you have a good chance of obtaining a refrigerator box by calling furniture stores that sell large appliances. Some of the activities below require a flashlight — you'll find flashlights in drug stores that cost only a few dollars.

INTRODUCTORY ACTIVITIES

ATTENTION GRABBER

Make the room as dark as you can. Close the curtains or blinds, and turn the lights off. If you have a candle, you may want to light it. Sit in a close group with the children, and ask them which is spookier — having the lights on and the curtains/blinds open, or having the room dark. Talk about the difference, and how it feels to be sitting together in the dark. If you're working with very young children, you may not want to make the room too dark — use your own judgment.

INTRODUCTORY DISCUSSION

objective   Introduce the theme, stimulate discussion and encourage language use.

materials   Rhyme

directions   Read the rhyme at least twice. Let the children know that "hither" means "here." Ask the children to make a creaking and groaning sound the way the wooden boards of an old floor might. Ask the children to howl and moan the way the wind might. Ask them to shiver the way they might if they were in a spooky house. Let the kids know that you'll be talking about spooky places for the next few days.

SOCIAL STUDIES: Talking About Fear

objective   Discuss fear and help children understand that fear is not bad; explore the idea that sometimes other people can help us through fear.

directions   Ask the children which they would prefer: to be in a dark room alone, or to be in a dark room with other people. If some kids say they would rather be with other people, ask them why. Ask the children if they've ever been scared, and ask them to share their experiences. Tell them about a time when you were scared, and when someone else helped you feel less afraid. Ask: "Do you think fear is bad?" Often, some children say they are never afraid. Talk about how fear can help us get out of dangerous situations. Say: "If something heavy was falling, and if I was afraid it would fall on me and that made me get out of the way really quickly, then it would be a good thing that I was afraid."

MUSIC/MOVEMENT:
The Spooky House Song

objective Help children enjoy singing; develop cognition through memorization of words and connected actions; develop imagination.

materials To the tune of The Wheels On The Bus, and using the words of the rhyme on the rhyme page:

The boards of the floor do creak and groan,
creak and groan, creak and groan.
The boards of the floor do creak and groan,
all through the spooky house.

The wind outside. . . and so forth.

directions Ask the children to sing the song in the slowest, deepest, spookiest voices they can. When you come to the words creak and groan, make your voices creak and groan. When you come to the words howl and moan, make your voices howl and moan. For "sticky cobwebs," move your fingers as if they're all tangled in sticky webs. For ". . . shifting shadows make you shiver," hug yourself and shiver. Sing the song first with the lights on, then close the blinds and curtains, turn the lights off, and sing the song again. You may decide not to do this if you work with younger children. Ask the children what else might happen in a Spooky House, and incorporate their ideas into the song by creating your own verses.

SCIENCE:
Fire Needs Air

objective Demonstrate to children that fire needs air; stimulate discussion; facilitate hypothesizing, experimenting, and communicating.

materials A candle
Matches
A glass
A plate or shallow container for the candle

preparation Light your candle and drip melted wax onto your plate or container. When enough wax has accumulated, stick the base of the candle in it, so that the candle stands upright.

directions After turning the lights off during introductory activities, light your candle. Ask the children what they think will happen if you put a glass over the candle. Encourage all the kids to hypothesize about this, and then have them take turns putting the glass over the candle. Some may want to experiment and simply hold the glass over the candle, rather than completely cover it. Relight the candle each time the flame is extinguished. When the flame goes out, ask the children why they think it did. Facilitate a discussion about this, and when appropriate, introduce the information that fire needs air to burn.

ACTIVITY CENTERS

ART/GROSS MOTOR:
Making A Spooky House

objective Develop creative expression; develop self-esteem by enabling children to decorate their own house; develop large muscles through the crouching, bending and stretching required to paint entire box.

materials A refrigerator box or other very large box
Different colors of paint
Fat brushes
A small table
An exacto knife

preparation Spread newspaper down on the floor, and put the box on top. Cut out a flap for a door. Put the paint and brushes on the table, and place it near the box.

directions Encourage the children to paint the spooky house. Keep your spooky house for other activities below.

ART:
Ghosts

objective Facilitate creative expression; develop fine motor skills.

materials Cardboard toilet paper rolls
An old sheet
Rubber bands
Markers
Newspaper

preparation Cut the old sheet into 5 1/2" squares. Take newspaper sheets, and squeeze pages into balls that will fit snugly into an end of a toilet paper roll. Make a ghost yourself by stuffing a newspaper ball into one paper roll end, and covering it with a sheet square. Secure the sheet by putting a rubber band over the cardboard roll, about where the ghost's neck would be. Draw a face onto it. Make several extras for the Ghost Count activity below. Arrange all the above materials on your work surface.

directions During one day's introductory activities, hold your ghost behind your back, and make a ghost sound. Ask the children to guess what kind of thing might make a noise like that. Show them your ghost, and let them hold it if they would like. Let them know that if they would like to make their own ghosts, that the materials are available on the work table. Either hang their ghosts up in the Spooky House, or, if the kids want to take their ghosts home, make extras and hang those up by tying them with white string and taping one end of the string onto the walls and ceiling of the Spooky House.

MATH:
Ghost Count

objective Facilitate rational counting; facilitate reading and writing.

materials Ghosts from above activity
A flashlight
Picture sign saying: "Would you like to count the ghosts in the Spooky House?"
Writing sheets that ask: "How many ghosts do you count in the Spooky House?"
Pen
Small table
Twine or string

preparation In this activity, the kids will be counting how many ghosts are hanging from the ceiling in Ye Olde Spooky House. Cut different lengths of string so that your ghosts hang down at different points. Use tacks or tape to secure them to the top of the box. Place the table near the door of Ye Olde Spooky House. Put the picture activity sign on it, and also photocopies of the writing sheets, pens, and flashlight.

directions If/when the children ask about the sign, help them interpret or 'read' it. Ahead of time, you may need to talk about the fact that there is only one flashlight, and that kids will have to take turns with it, when they go inside Ye Olde Spooky House to count the ghosts. Invite the children to use the writing sheets to write down how many ghosts they counted.

LANGUAGE/ART:
Spooky House Stories

objective Develop all components of language: reading, writing, speaking and listening.

materials
Black construction paper
White construction paper
Markers
Glue sticks
Magazines
White chalk

preparation Using the pattern on page 209, or a variation of it, cut out Spooky House shapes from black construction paper. Go through magazines, and cut out pictures of people from diverse cultures and lifestyles. If you're working with children 4 years and older, you may just want to tear pages out and let the kids do the cutting. Make your own Spooky House story. There are a variety of ways to do it: Glue the black Spooky House shape onto white paper, or not. Glue photos of people inside the windows and doors, or not. Use markers to draw on the white paper, or use chalk to draw on the black house. However you make yours, write a story about your Spooky House on your final creation. Arrange all materials on a work table.

directions During introductory activities, show the children your Spooky House, and read them the story. Let them know that if they would like to make their own Spooky House story, that the materials are available on a work table. Take story dictation, encourage the kids to write their own words, or write down their words for them to copy. After the day's activities, gather together again and ask the kids if anyone would like to show and read their Spooky House stories.

DRAMATIC PLAY/SENSORY:
Ye Olde Spooky House

objective Facilitate creative and imaginative play; facilitate child-to-child interactions; facilitate sensory exploration of dark and light.

materials
Ye Olde Spooky House (made in above art activity)
Flashlight
Timer (optional)

preparation   During introductory activities, reinforce once again, that there's only one flashlight, and that kids will have to take turns with it. Depending on the number of children you're working with, or their ages, you may need a timer.

directions   Encourage the children to explore the spooky house. (My experience has been that no encouragement is needed. My children usually spend a huge amount of time just sitting in the box, playing and giggling and talking.)

EXTENDING THE CONCEPT

art   With packing boxes, shoe boxes, smaller boxes, strawberry baskets, spools, and other materials you gather, make a miniature Spooky House as a group project. Paint or decorate it in a spooky way.

dramatic play   With Fisher Price wooden people, or other small doll figures, encourage the children to use the Spooky House they made in the above activity as a doll house.

cognitive   Play a group game with a ghost. One child waits in Ye Olde Spooky House, and one child hides a ghost behind someone's back. The person in Ye Olde Spooky House comes out and tries to guess who's hiding a ghost behind her/his back.

LITERATURE

Berenstain, Stan & Jan, *The Spooky Old Tree*, Random House, 1978
Benchley, Nathaniel, *A Ghost Named Fred*, Harper & Row, 1968 (This is a wonderful story, but beware of the illustration of the pirate with the eye-patch. Either talk to the children about the fact that people they see with eye patches are not bad people or pirates, or skip the page.)
Noodles, *How To Catch A Ghost*, Holt, Rinehart & Winston, 1979 (Talk to the kids about which places in the book look spooky and why.)

**Whingy whiner
gripes and groans,
frowns and glowers,
mewls and moans.**

whingy whiner

This theme helps children understand that what are traditionally viewed as negative emotions (disappointment, frustration, anger) are in fact, human and normal. This unit aims on building acceptance of these feelings. ("Whinge" is an Irish word, and means a whimpering whine. "Whingy" is pronounced the same as the word "windy," except with a soft g -as in hinge- instead of a d.)

INTRODUCTORY ACTIVITIES

ATTENTION GRABBER

After all the children are gathered, tell them that you're going to make a face, and that you want them to guess what you're feeling. Smile. Look worried. Look excited. Look sad. Then tell the kids that voices can also tell us something about what

217

people feel. Use the sentence: "I'm going to use that marker." Say it in an excited way, an angry way, a whiny way. Encourage the children to guess each time, what it is you might be feeling if you said it that way.

INTRODUCTORY DISCUSSION

objective   Introduce the theme; encourage discussion; expand vocabulary.

materials   Rhyme page

directions   Read the rhyme at least twice. Go over each word and demonstrate what it means if the children don't already know. A mewl is a very weak whimper or whine. To glower means to stare with sullen anger; to scowl. Ask the children what kinds of things they think the Whingy Whiner whines about.

SOCIAL STUDIES:
Feelings

objective   Help children accept painful feelings such as frustration, disappointment, anger; help kids accept themselves when they feel these emotions.

directions   Make a frown or glower, and ask the kids what they think you would be feeling if you looked that way. When the children say "angry," ask them if it's O.K. to be angry. Talk about other feelings, like frustration and disappointment, in the same way. Share an experience with the children in which you felt one or more of these emotions. Ask them if they can remember a time when they felt one of these things. Encourage them to verbalize their experiences. Reinforce the fact that all the above feelings are feelings that everyone feels at some time or another, and that it's O.K. to feel them.

SCIENCE/SENSORY:
Face Muscles

objective   Facilitate an understanding that we have muscles in our faces and that those muscles control our expressions; facilitate sensory exploration of facial expressions with fingertips.

directions   Ask the children to make various expressions: a happy look, a sad look, an angry look, a worried look. Ask them to use their fingertips to feel their cheeks, lips, chins and foreheads while they make these faces. Encourage them to keep their fingertips on their faces and foreheads while they change expressions. Ask them: "Do you feel your skin move? Do you feel the muscles underneath your skin?" Ask them to smile the biggest smile they can, and to feel their cheeks at the same time. Talk about the muscles that make our cheeks puff out when we smile.

MUSIC/MOVEMENT:
I Lost My Purple Lollipop

objective   Help children enjoy singing; develop cognition through memorization of words and connected actions.

materials   To the tune of Froggie Went A-Courting:
"I lost my purple lollipop, I did, I did.
I lost my purple lollipop, I did —
I looked up and I looked down;
Couldn't find it, so I frowned, I did, I did.

I finally found my lollipop, I did, I did.
I finally found my lollipop, I did.
I looked and looked a long, long while;
finally found it, so I smiled, I did, I did.

It had a piece of fluff on it, it did, it did.
It had a piece of fluff on it, it did.
That piece of fluff was stuck right down,
wouldn't come off; it made me frown, it did, it did.

I washed my lollipop all off, I did, I did.
I washed my lollipop all off, I did.
I washed it off a long, long while;
the fluff came off; it made me smile, it did, it did!

directions   For: "I lost my purple lollipop," hold your hands out in an "I don't have it" gesture. Pantomime looking up and looking down, and frown during last line of first verse. For "I finally found my lollipop," pretend to hold a lollipop. For "I looked and looked a long, long while," put your hand over your eyebrows and move your head from right to left. Smile during the last line of the second verse. For "It had a piece of fluff on it," pretend to touch a piece of fluff with your thumb and forefinger. For "That piece of fluff was stuck right down, wouldn't come off," pretend to try to pull it off. Frown for the last line of the third verse. For "I washed my lollipop all off," pantomime washing off a lollipop under a faucet. Smile for the last line of the fourth verse. After the song ask: "What should we do with our lollipops?" If you like, pretend to eat them.

ACTIVITY CENTERS

ART:
Whingy Whiner Puppets

objective   Facilitate creative expression; promote self-esteem and sense of autonomy by providing choices; develop fine motor skills.

materials   Whingy Whiner pattern on page 217
Tagboard/construction paper
Wide tongue depressors (medical offices will sometimes donate these)
Glue
Glue brushes
Markers
Yarn
Beads
Collage paper scraps
Macaroni
Buttons
Fabric scraps

preparation   Photocopy and cut out enough Whingy Whiner shapes from tagboard or construction paper for all your children. Arrange all the materials on a table. Make your own Whingy Whiner puppet ahead of time by covering the shape with whatever materials you choose, and gluing your whiner onto a tongue depressor so you can use it as a puppet. To keep this project open-ended, have tagboard or construction paper pieces available that haven't been cut into any specific shape so that children can create their own shapes and take the project in their own directions if they desire.

directions   On the day that you're doing this activity, bring out your Whiner puppet during Attention Grabber time. Make your puppet whine about anything you like and try to stimulate a reaction to, and interaction with, the Whiner from the children. Show them the materials on the table, and encourage them to make their own puppets. Explain that they will have to glue their puppets onto the sticks another day, after the glue has dried on their Whingy Whiners.

DRAMATIC PLAY:
Whingy Whiner Puppets

objective   Promote pretending and imaginative play; develop coordination of action with speech; facilitate self-expression; generate enthusiasm for dramatic arts.

materials   Puppet theater
Whingy Whiner puppets from above activity
Chairs

preparation   If you don't have a puppet theater, turn a small table over on its side, or hang a broom across the backs of two chairs and hang a tablecloth over it. Arrange some chairs in front of the theater for the audience. During an Attention Grabber time, use your Whiner puppet in the theater to talk to the children and to whine about things in general. Then invite children to use their puppets in the theater also. Spend some time sitting in a chair as an audience to children's dramatic play.

ART/LANGUAGE:
Feelings Book

objective   Help children consciously differentiate between emotions; help children connect facial expressions with emotions; facilitate creative expression; develop all components of language: reading, writing, speaking, listening.

materials   Magazines
Construction paper
Markers
Scissors
Glue sticks

preparation   Make blank books by folding two pages over, and stapling along the fold. If you're working with young children, leaf through magazines and cut out photographs of people from diverse cultures and lifestyles who are displaying different emotions. Look specifically for expressions that seem frustrated, disappointed, angry. If you're working with older kids, you can tear the pages out and let the kids cut the faces out themselves. Spread all materials on a work surface. Make your own feelings book. Make a design for the cover and also write the title and author on it. Choose faces that have interesting expressions on them and glue them in the pages, or draw your own faces, and write a few words about each one.

directions   During introductory activities, read your feelings book to the children. Discuss the faces in your book. Let the kids know that if they would like to make their own feelings book, the materials are available on a table. Take story dictation when appropriate, or write down the children's words for them to copy. Read the children's stories back to them and/or encourage them to read their words to you.

MATH:
Whingy Whiner Board

objective Develop sense of autonomy through one-person work station; facilitate rational counting; facilitate matching activity; develop all components of language: speaking, listening, reading and writing.

materials
Whingy Whiner from 217
One side of a large cardboard box, or foam core
Writing sheets (described below)
Pens
Double-sided tape or glue
Construction paper (seven or eight different colors)
Contact paper
Teacher/Parent puppet
A "One Person May Be Here" sign
Picture sign saying: "Would you like to count the Whingy Whiners under the flaps?"
A one-person work table
Exacto knife
Scissors

preparation In this activity, you're going to hide different colors of removable Whingy Whiners underneath matching colored flaps on a board, and the children will count and match them. From seven or eight colors of construction paper, cut out one flap from each sheet. The size of your flaps should depend on how many whiners you'll be hiding underneath, which will depend on how high your children count. Also, you'll have to decide how many flaps your foam core or cardboard can accommodate. Glue these flaps onto your board. Make many photocopies of the Whingy Whiner from the pattern on page 217. (Again, the number should depend on how high your kids can count. Unless you have time, there's no need to thoroughly color in each whingy whiner. Just take a fat crayon and quickly scribble or color lightly each whiner, making sure that you have several of each color to correspond with the color of flaps. After you've colored your whiners, and before you cut any out, cover each sheet of paper on both sides with contact paper, and then cut out each whiner. If you want to save time, you can cut around the whiners rather than cut each actual shape. However, this activity seems to grab more interest from kids if the actual whiners are cut out, and a fast way to do this is to put several sheets on top of each other, and then do your cutting. Put strips of double-sided tape under each flap, and stick on the whiners that correspond in color. In marker, also write that number (of whiners) under each flap. On the top of the board write: "How Many Whingy Whiners?" To make the writing sheets, write the sentence "How many (color) Whingy Whiners do you count?" for each color you've made, inserting the names of the colors in the sentences as appropriate. Put a scribble of the appropriate color over the color word after you've photocopied the sheets. Set out the "One Person May Be Here" sign.

directions Encourage the kids to use the materials. Take out your puppet and through the puppet's personality, ask each child who explores the materials about what he/she is doing.

GROSS MOTOR:
Whingy Whiner Fishing

objective Facilitate hand/eye coordination; develop large muscles.

materials Photocopies of Whingy Whiner
Juice can lids
Double-sided tape
Picture sign saying: "Would you like to fish for Whingy Whiners?"
Magnetic fishing rods (used in Gizmo Fishing activity, page 186)

preparation After cutting out ten or twelve whiners, use double-sided tape to stick one onto each juice can lid. Spread these out on the ground, and put the magnetic fishing rods and activity sign nearby.

directions Invite the kids to fish for Whingy Whiners. Sincerely praise all efforts.

EXTENDING THE CONCEPT

music/ cognitive When singing the lollipop song, try singing it and leaving out the word "lollipop." It's fun to see if you can remember not to say a word that occurs frequently in a song.

art Provide all the materials listed in the language activity, and encourage the children to make their own Whingy Whiner houses. Then let them tell their own stories with their materials during introductory group activities.

LITERATURE

*Castle, Sue, *Face Talk, Hand Talk, Body Talk*, Doubleday & Co., 1977
*Viorst, Judith, *Alexander And The Terrible, Horrible, No Good, Very Bad Day*, Aladdin Books, 1972 (Read this story once, then go back and look at Alexander's facial expression on each page. Ask the children what his face tells about what he's feeling.)
*McGovern, Ann, *Feeling Mad, Feeling Sad, Feeling Bad, Feeling Glad*, Magic Circle Press, 1977

RESOURCES

RESOURCE BOOKS FOR MULTICULTURALISM

Slapin, Beverly and Doris Seale, *Through Indian Eyes; The Native Experience In Books For Children*, New Society Publishers

Slapin, Beverly and Doris Seale, *How To Tell The Difference; A Checklist For Evaluating Children's Books For Anti-Indian Bias*, New Society Publishers

Kruse, Ginny Moore and Kathleen T. Horning, *Multicultural Literature For Children And Young Adults; A Selected Listing Of Books 1980-1990 By And About People Of Color*, Cooperative Children's Book Center

Sims, Rudine, Shadow And Substance, *Afro-American Experience In Contemporary Children's Fiction*, National Council Of Teachers Of English

Lindgren, Merri V., *The Multicolored Mirror; Cultural Substance In Literature For Children And Young Adults*, Cooperative Children's Book Center/Highsmith Press

Miller-Lachmann, Lyn, *Our Family Our Friends Our World*, R.R. Bowker Company

SUPPLY COMPANIES

Multicultural Instruments

Asian Cooking Set (Expensive: around $80)
Latino Cooking Set (Expensive: around $70)
Childcraft
20 Kilmer Road
Post Office Box 3081
Edison, NJ 08818-3081
1-800-631-5652

Balls and buttons

Kaplan School Supply Corp.
1310 Lewisville-Clemmons Rd.
P.O. Box 609
Lewisville, NC 27023-0609

Buttons

Lakeshore Learning Materials
2695 E. Dominguez St.
Carson, CA 90749
1-800-421-5354

Sewing Basket

ABC School Supply Inc
3312 N. Berkeley Lake Road
P.O. Box 100019
Duluth, GA 30136
1-800-669-4ABC

FLANNEL BOARDS

Sook and the Lost Button

Sook and the Lost Button

The Sun and the Dinosaurs

The Magic Water Well

The Magic Water Well

There Was a Peanut

Old Goat Tucker

Ms. Gizmo

CLIP ART

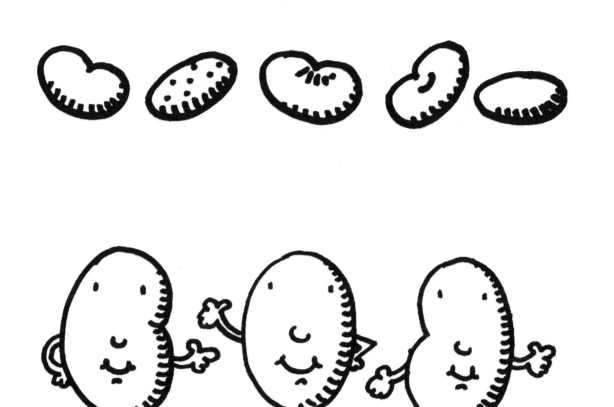

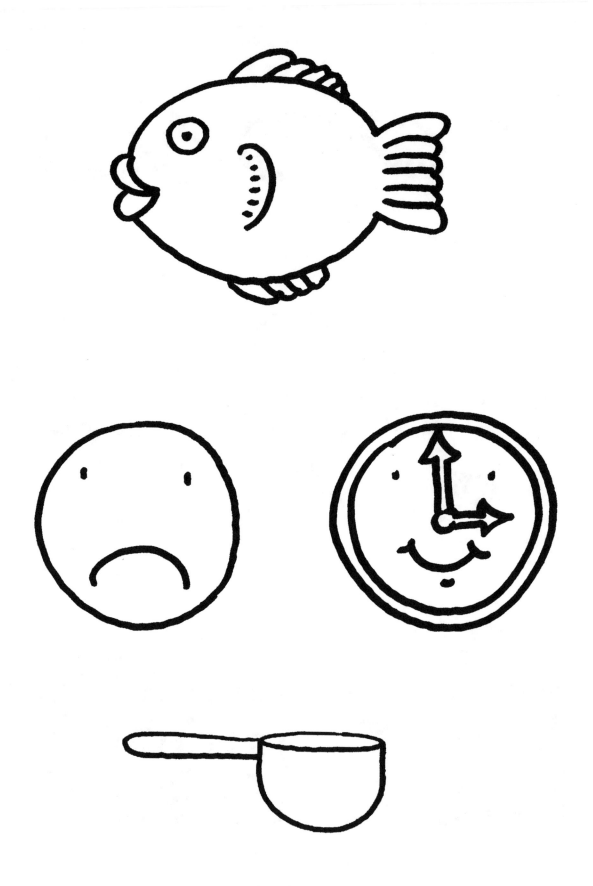